Why did the tomato turn red?

Because it saw the
salad dressing!

# ALL MY FAVORITE RECIPES

# ALL MY FAVORITE RECIPES, WITH A HINT OF GIGGLE

Dr. Constance Santego

Maximillian Enterprises
Kelowna, BC

*All My Favorite Recipes, With A Hint Of Giggle*
*Copyright © 2023 by Dr. Constance Santego.*

Copy Editor and Interior Design: Constance Santego
Book Layout: ©2017 BookDesignTemplates.com
Cover Design: Constance Santego

Ordering Information:
Quantity sales. Special discounts are available on quantity purchases by corporations, associations, and others.

Trade paperback ISBN: 978-1-990062-10-0

eBook ISBN 978-1-990062-11-7

Created and published In Canada. Printed and bound in the United States of America

Second Edition
Published by Maximillian Enterprises
Kelowna, BC
Canada
www.constancesantego.ca

# Dedication
## To My Children and Grandbabies

"May your taste buds forever be delighted, your rest always soothing, your achievements countless, your journey through life be filled with boundless joy, unwavering love, and the courage to chase your dreams with all your heart."

## Love GiGi

What do you call a tech-savvy grandma?

A "gigabyte" of wisdom!

# ALSO BY DR. CONSTANCE SANTEGO

**FICTION**
**The Nine Spiritual Gifts Series:**

Journey of a Soul – (Vol. 1 Michael)
Language of a Soul – (Vol. 2 Gabriel)
Prophecy of a Soul – (Vol. 3 Bath Kol)
Healing of a Soul – (Vol. 4 Raphael)

**NON-FICTION**
The Intuitive Life, The Gift of Prophecy, Third Edition
Fairy Tales, Dreams and Reality… Where Are You On Your Path? Second Edition
Your Persona… The Mask You Wear
Angelic Lifestyle, A Vibrant Lifestyle
Angelic Lifestyle 42-Day Energy Cleanse
Archangel Michael's Soul Retrieval Guide

**SECRETS OF A HEALER, SERIES:**

Magic of Aromatherapy (Vol. I)
Magic of Reflexology (Vol. II)
Magic of The Gifts (Vol. III)
Magic of Muscle Testing (Vol. IV)
Magic of Iridology (Vol. V)
Magic of Massage (Vol. VI)
Magic of Hypnotherapy (Vol. VII)
Magic of Reiki (Vol. VIII)
Magic of Advanced Aromatherapy (Vol. IX)
Magic of Esthetics (Vol. X)

**FOR CHILDREN**

I am big tonight. I don't need the light!

What did the lettuce say
to the celery?

"Are you stalking
me?"

ALL MY FAVORITE RECIPES

What's an appetizer's favorite
part of a book?

The table of
contents!

# Contents

What did the cake say to the fork?

"You want a piece of me?"

# *Preface*

Once upon a time, in a world where flavors danced and aromas enchanted, there lived a young girl named Connie. At the tender age of ten, Connie had already developed an extraordinary passion for food—exploring markets, experimenting with recipes, and savoring every taste sensation that came her way. Food was not just sustenance for Connie; it was a magical journey of discovery that filled her heart with joy and wonder.

Every meal was a cherished adventure for Connie, and her love for cooking sparked joyous gatherings of family and friends. From crafting playful cupcakes to daringly delicious dishes, Connie's kitchen was a realm of culinary delights. However, life had a surprise in store for her that would test her determination and reshape her culinary path.

Later in life, at the age of fifty, Connie faced a new chapter in her culinary journey. Her love for food had been a constant companion throughout her years, shaping her experiences and connecting her with cherished memories. However, life had a surprise in store for her—a diagnosis of diabetes that would alter the way she approached her passion.

Connie had always been an adventurous soul in the kitchen, fearlessly experimenting with flavors and delighting in the art of creating exquisite dishes. Her meals were a reflection of her vibrant spirit, and she took joy in sharing her culinary creations with family and friends.

The news that she had been diagnosed with diabetes was met with a mix of emotions, as she grappled with the idea that the very thing, she loved most could now pose challenges to her health. The flavors that once brought joy were now intertwined with the need for careful consideration.

With the support of her loved ones and her own resilience, Connie embarked on a journey to understand diabetes and its impact on her culinary world. Armed with knowledge and determination, she navigated the intricacies of managing her condition while continuing to indulge in her passion for food. Sugars, once her sweet companions, now required mindful moderation. Carbohydrates, once enjoyed without restraint, became part of a balanced equation for her well-being.

Undeterred by the changes, Connie embraced her new reality with grace and innovation. She adapted recipes, explored alternative ingredients, and found ingenious ways to infuse flavors into her dishes without compromising her health. Every cooking session became an opportunity to explore, learn, and evolve her culinary techniques.

Through this journey, Connie's relationship with food deepened even further. Each dish she crafted was a testament to her strength, adaptability, and unwavering spirit. The joy of cooking remained a constant source of inspiration, and her determination to savor life's flavors became a beacon of hope for those around her.

The story of Connie's love for food and her unexpected encounter with diabetes became a tale of resilience, transformation, and the enduring power of passion. It served as a reminder that life's challenges could be met with courage and that the pursuit of joy could be reimagined in the face of change. As Connie continued to explore her culinary path, her story illuminated the way for others, showing that no matter the circumstances, the love for food could remain a source of inspiration and connection throughout life's journey.

P.S. In 2003, we were evacuated from our home due to a forest fire. As I write this, twenty years later, we are on evacuation alert for another forest fire. Dad and I spent a few weeks at nan's and once I was at home (yes, still under the alert) I decided that I want "All My Favorite Recipes" in one cookbook. A book that no matter what happens I can order another one.

*Enjoy, GiGi (Dr. Constance)*

What's a dessert's favorite clothing?

The one with sprinkles!

"I'm on a seafood diet.

I see food, and I
eat it!"

# *Dear Cook*

Welcome to a culinary journey that combines the art of cooking with the essence of life's twists and turns. Within the pages of this cookbook, you'll find more than just recipes; you'll uncover stories of resilience, passion, and the unbreakable bond between flavors and the human spirit.

As you explore these recipes, remember that each dish has a tale to tell. From the pages of this cookbook emerges a narrative of love for food, creativity in the face of challenges, and the joy of sharing nourishment with those we hold dear. It's a journey that transcends the kitchen and reaches into the heart of what it means to truly savor life's flavors.

Whether you're a seasoned chef or an aspiring home cook, these recipes are crafted with care to ignite your passion and ignite your creativity. Let the aromas fill your kitchen, and the stories fill your soul. Just as the characters in these tales have overcome obstacles and embraced change, may you find inspiration to infuse every meal with your own unique blend of determination and love.

So, venture forth into these culinary narratives, and let your senses be your guide. Discover the stories behind the recipes, the dedication that has gone into each creation, and the triumphs that can emerge from unexpected twists. As you cook and share these dishes, may they not only satisfy your appetite but also remind you of the resilience and beauty that lie within every culinary masterpiece.

With gratitude for joining us on this flavorful adventure,
Shift happens…Create magic!

Dr. Constance Santego

What do you call cheese that
isn't yours?

Nacho cheese!

# Measurement Quick Conversion

| | | | |
|---|---|---|---|
| 1/8 Teaspoon | 0.625 ml | Dash or pinch | |
| ¼ Teaspoon | 1.25 ml | | |
| ½ Teaspoon | 2.5 ml | | |
| 1 Teaspoon | 5 ml | 5 grams | |
| 3 Teaspoons | 15 ml | 1/16 cup | 1 Tablespoon |
| 1 Tablespoon | 15 ml | 1/16 cup | 3 Teaspoons |
| 2 Tablespoons | 31.25 ml | 1/8 cup | |
| 4 Tablespoons | 62.5 ml | ¼ cup | |
| 8 Tablespoons | 125 ml | ½ cup | 1 stick of butter |
| 12 tablespoons | 187.5 ml | ¾ cup | |
| 16 Tablespoons | 250 ml | 1 cup | 8 ounces, ½ pint or ½ pound |
| 32 Tablespoons | 500 ml | 2 cups | ½ liter, 1 pound/lb |
| 64 Tablespoons | 1 liter | 4 cups | 2 pints or 1 quart |
| 256 Tablespoons | 4 liters | 16 cups | 8 pints, 4 quarts or 1 gallon |

Milliliters measure volume, while pounds measure weight. The conversion between volume and weight depends on the density of the substance you are measuring. Comparisons are approximate.

# Abbreviations

Tsp (tsp) = Teaspoon

Tbsp (tbsp) = Tablespoon

C = Cup

Lb = pound

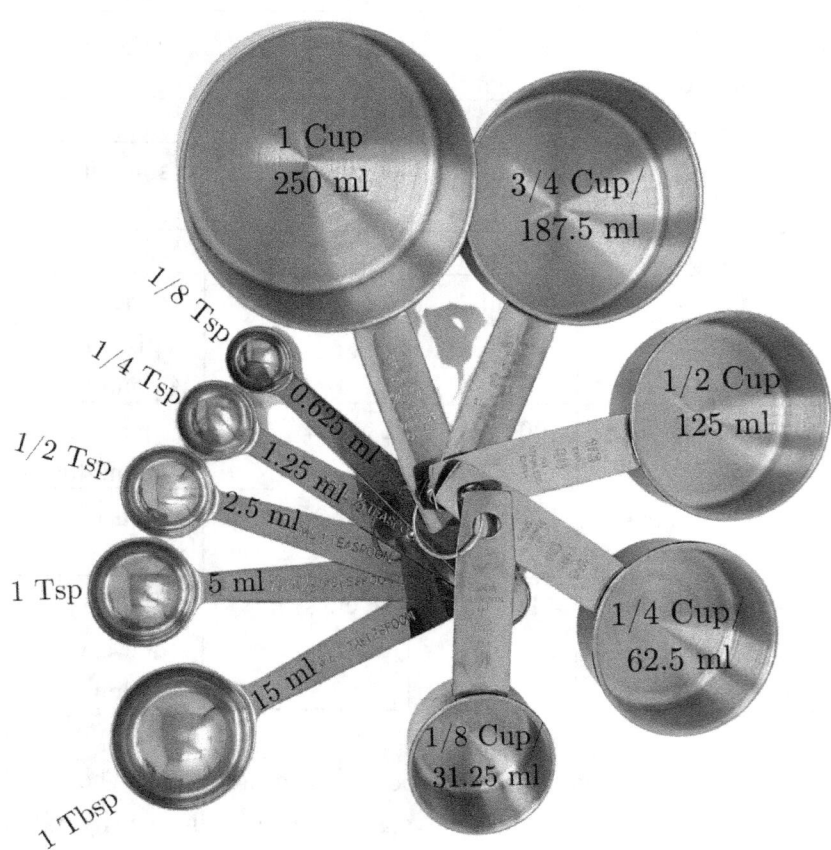

# Safe Cooking Temperatures

Cook foods to the recommended safe minimum internal temperature listed below.

Beef & Veal

| | | |
|---|---|---|
| Ground | 160 °F | |
| Steak and roasts medium | | 160 °F |
| Steak and roasts medium rare | 145 °F | |

Chicken & Turkey

| | | |
|---|---|---|
| Breasts | | 165 °F |
| Ground, stuffing, and casserole | 165 °F | |
| Whole bird, legs, thighs, and wings | | 165 °F |

Eggs

| | |
|---|---|
| Any type | 160 °F |

Fish & Shellfish

| | |
|---|---|
| Any type | 145 °F |

Lamb

| | | |
|---|---|---|
| Ground | 160 °F | |
| Steak and roasts medium | | 160 °F |
| Steak and roasts medium rare | 145 °F | |

Leftovers

| | |
|---|---|
| Any type | 165 °F |

Pork

| | | |
|---|---|---|
| Chops, fresh (raw) ham ground, ribs and roasts | 160 °F | |
| Fully cooked ham (to reheat) | | 140 °F |

# Bread Alternatives

When considering bread options for diabetics, it's important to focus on those with lower carbohydrate content and a lower glycemic index to help manage blood sugar levels. Here are some bread alternatives to sourdough that can be suitable for diabetics:

- **Whole Grain Bread:** Opt for whole-grain bread made from whole wheat, oats, or other whole grains. These types of bread generally have more fiber, which can help slow down the digestion of carbohydrates and prevent rapid spikes in blood sugar.
- **Sprouted Grain Bread:** Sprouted grain bread is made from whole grains that have been allowed to sprout before being used in baking. This process can increase the availability of nutrients and reduce the carbohydrate content.
- **100% Whole Wheat Bread:** Look for bread that is labeled as "100% whole wheat" to ensure it is made entirely from whole wheat flour without added refined flour.
- **Low-Carb Bread:** Some specialty breads are specifically marketed as low-carb options for people watching their carbohydrate intake. These breads are often made with alternative flours like almond flour, coconut flour, or flaxseed meal.
- **Flaxseed Bread:** Bread made with flaxseed meal is high in fiber and healthy fats, making it a good option for diabetics. It also has a lower glycemic index compared to traditional bread.
- **Almond Flour Bread:** Bread made with almond flour is low in carbohydrates and rich in healthy fats and protein. It's a great choice for those looking to reduce their carb intake.
- **Coconut Flour Bread:** Similar to almond flour bread, coconut flour bread is low in carbs and provides added fiber and healthy fats.
- **Rye Bread (Whole Grain or Pumpernickel):** Rye bread, especially whole grain or pumpernickel varieties, can have a lower glycemic index compared to some other breads. However, portion control is important, as rye bread can still affect blood sugar levels.

- **Ezekiel Bread:** Ezekiel bread is made from sprouted grains and legumes, providing a good balance of protein, fiber, and complex carbohydrates.
- **Homemade Bread Alternatives:** Consider making your own bread using alternative flours like almond, coconut, or flaxseed. There are many diabetic-friendly recipes available online that cater to different dietary preferences.

When selecting bread, always read the nutritional labels to check the carbohydrate and fiber content. It's also a good idea to monitor your blood sugar levels after trying a new bread to see how it affects you personally. Remember that moderation is key, and consulting with a healthcare professional or registered dietitian can help you make informed choices that align with your individual health goals and dietary needs.

# Bun/Muffin Alternatives

For individuals with diabetes looking to reduce their carbohydrate intake, there are several low-carb and diabetes-friendly alternatives to traditional English muffins in Eggs Benedict. Here are some options:

1. **Portobello Mushrooms:** Use grilled or roasted portobello mushroom caps as a base instead of English muffins. They have a meaty texture and can hold the other ingredients well.
2. **Eggplant Slices:** Roasted or grilled eggplant slices can serve as a flavorful and low-carb base for Eggs Benedict. They provide a unique texture and absorb the flavors of the other ingredients.
3. **Zucchini or Cucumber Slices:** Thinly sliced zucchini or cucumber rounds can be a refreshing and low-carb alternative. You can lightly sauté or grill them for added flavor.
4. **Cauliflower "English Muffins":** Make cauliflower-based English muffins or rounds by combining cauliflower rice with egg, cheese, and seasoning. Bake these in muffin tins to create a low-carb base.
5. **Lettuce Leaves:** Large lettuce leaves, such as butter lettuce or iceberg lettuce, can be used as a crunchy and low-carb wrap for Eggs Benedict. They add a refreshing crunch to each bite.
6. **Avocado Halves**: Scoop out a small portion of an avocado half to create a well for the poached egg. It adds a creamy and nutritious base.
7. **Gluten-Free or Low-Carb Bread**: There are gluten-free and low-carb bread options available in stores that are suitable for diabetics. Look for bread made with almond flour, coconut flour, or flaxseed meal.

When choosing any of these alternatives, it's essential to keep portion control in mind, as even low-carb options can impact blood sugar levels. Additionally, pair your Eggs Benedict with a source of protein and plenty of non-starchy vegetables to create a balanced and diabetes-friendly meal.

# Sugar Alternatives

People with diabetes need to be cautious about their sugar intake to manage their blood glucose levels. There are several sugar alternatives and sweeteners that are commonly used by diabetics, as they have little to no impact on blood sugar levels. Some of these include:

1. **Stevia:** Derived from the leaves of the stevia plant, stevia is a natural sweetener that does not raise blood sugar levels.
2. **Monk Fruit Extract:** Monk fruit extract, also known as monk fruit sweetener, is a natural sweetener that comes from the monk fruit. It contains no calories or carbohydrates and does not affect blood sugar.
3. **Erythritol:** Erythritol is a sugar alcohol that is often used as a sugar substitute. It provides sweetness without causing a significant increase in blood sugar levels and has fewer calories than regular sugar.
4. **Xylitol:** Xylitol is another sugar alcohol that is commonly used as a sugar substitute. It has a minimal impact on blood sugar levels and is often used in sugar-free gum and toothpaste.
5. **Agave Nectar:** While it has a lower glycemic index compared to regular sugar, agave nectar should still be consumed in moderation as it can still affect blood sugar levels.

It's important for individuals with diabetes to monitor their blood sugar levels and consult with their healthcare provider or a registered dietitian before incorporating any new sweeteners into their diet. Everyone's response to sweeteners can vary, so it's essential to find the options that work best for each individual's needs and preferences.

# Meat Cooking Times

The cooking time for meats can vary widely depending on the type of meat, its thickness, the cooking method, and the desired level of doneness. Here are some general guidelines for cooking various meats:

**Beef:**

1. Steak (1-inch thick): For medium-rare, cook for 3-4 minutes per side. Add a minute or two for medium and well-done.
2. Ground Beef: Cook ground beef until it reaches an internal temperature of 160°F (71°C).
3. Roasts: Roasting times vary based on the cut and weight. A general guideline is to roast beef at 325°F (163°C) for about 20-25 minutes per pound for medium-rare. Use a meat thermometer to check for doneness.

**Pork:**

1. Pork Chops (1-inch thick): Cook for 4-5 minutes per side for medium. Pork should reach an internal temperature of 145°F (63°C).
2. Pork Tenderloin: Roast at 425°F (218°C) for about 20-25 minutes or until the internal temperature reaches 145°F (63°C).

**Chicken:**

1. Chicken Breasts (boneless and skinless): Cook for 6-8 minutes per side at medium-high heat or until the internal temperature reaches 165°F (74°C).
2. Whole Chicken: Roast at 350°F (177°C). A 3-4 pound chicken takes about 1.5 to 2 hours to cook.

**Fish:**

1.  Salmon: Bake at 375°F (190°C) for 12-15 minutes per inch of thickness. Salmon is done when it flakes easily with a fork.
2.  Tilapia or Cod: Cook for 10-12 minutes per inch of thickness at 400°F (204°C).

Remember that these are just general guidelines. The best way to ensure that your meat is cooked to your liking and is safe to eat is by using a meat thermometer. Measure the internal temperature at the thickest part of the meat and refer to recommended safe temperatures for each type of meat. Cooking times can also vary based on your specific cooking equipment and conditions, so it's always a good idea to monitor your meat closely, especially if you're trying a new recipe or cooking method.

What did the sushi say to the bee?

"Wasabi!"

# Our Family History

The history of my family is a rich tapestry woven with diverse threads from all corners of the globe. According to what I've discovered on Ancestry.ca, we are Hintz 57—a captivating blend of nationalities that has shaped our unique identity.

On my mother's side, our roots stretch to the Czech Republic and Hungary, where the vibrant cultures of Central Europe have influenced our heritage. My maternal grandmother hails from these lands, carrying with her the traditions and flavors that have enriched our family.

My maternal grandfather's lineage weaves an intricate tapestry of backgrounds, combining French, Italian, Spanish, and Indigenous ancestry. This eclectic mix has undoubtedly left an indelible mark on our family's identity, with a diversity of influences that enrich our heritage.

On my father's side, our heritage is predominantly English, with traces of Irish and Scottish lineage adding a touch of Celtic charm to our story. This blend of cultures and traditions has shaped our family's journey through time.

Our family's journey to the Okanagan region in 1944 and 1912 for my mother's and father's sides, respectively, marked a significant chapter in our history. The decision to settle in this picturesque landscape undoubtedly contributed to the vibrant tapestry of experiences that define us today.

Food has always been the centerpiece of our family gatherings, nurturing not just our bodies but also our bonds. From fish on Fridays to expansive Christmas celebrations, our traditions have centered around sharing meals and creating memories with over fifty relatives. For us, food is synonymous with love—it's a language that transcends borders and generations.

The culinary legacy within our family is a treasure trove of talent. Grandparents, aunties, and uncles have gifted us with their culinary prowess, creating dishes that speak to the heart and nourish the soul. Their culinary artistry has passed down through the generations, leaving an imprint on our tastes and traditions.

As I reflect on our family's journey through time, it's evident that our roots are as diverse as they are deep. Our blend of nationalities, cultures, and culinary traditions has shaped us into a family that celebrates our differences and finds unity in the shared joy of food. Just as each ingredient contributes to a harmonious recipe, our family's history is a mosaic of experiences that come together to form a beautiful and unique whole.

The Okanagan Valley, nestled in the picturesque landscape of British Columbia, Canada, has a history as vibrant and varied as its landscapes. Over the years, this region has seen remarkable transformations that reflect its rich agricultural heritage and evolving cultural tapestry.

Once known for its tobacco fields that stretched across the valley, the Okanagan was a hub of agricultural activity. The fertile soil nurtured an abundance of crops, including the juicy fruits that have become synonymous with the region. From apples to cherries, the valley's orchards bore the fruits of labor and love, adding a burst of color and flavor to its surroundings.

But the Okanagan wasn't just about farming; it was a place where people came to bask in the warmth of the sun and revel in the delights of outdoor activities. Fun in the sun was a way of life, attracting visitors and locals alike to its inviting shores and breathtaking vistas.

Growing up in Kelowna, I've witnessed firsthand the winds of change that have swept through the Okanagan. The shift from vast farmlands to modern high rises marks a transformation that mirrors the changing times. The landscape evolved as urbanization took root, and the region embraced progress while preserving its natural beauty.

Among the significant shifts in the Okanagan's identity, the emergence of grapes as the valley's flagship fruit stands out prominently. The establishment of exceptional wineries transformed the region into a viticultural haven. Vineyards adorned the hillsides, and the art of winemaking blossomed, drawing enthusiasts from near and far to savor the exquisite flavors of Okanagan wines.

The transition from tobacco fields to bountiful orchards and now to world-class wineries is a testament to the Okanagan's resilience and adaptability. It has seamlessly blended its agricultural heritage with contemporary pursuits, creating a mosaic of traditions that pay homage to the past while embracing the present.

As I reflect on the evolution of the Okanagan Valley, it's a reminder that change is a constant companion on our journey through life. The valley's story mirrors the ebb and flow of time, where growth and transformation pave the way for new experiences and opportunities. Through it all, the Okanagan's allure endures—a place where history, nature, and progress harmonize to create a tapestry that is uniquely its own.

What do you call a fake noodle?

An "impasta"!

# Happiness Recipe

 Given to me by my cousin Coli as a wedding gift. *I still have the recipe box it came in.*

## Ingredients:

- 1 cup of friendship
- 2 cups of care
- 2 cups of love
- 1 cup of understanding
- 1 cup of good thoughts towards others
- 1 tablespoon of help
- 2 tablespoons of generosity
- 3 tablespoons of laughter
- 1 teaspoon of happy memories
- 2 teaspoons of smiles
- 1 pinch of hope

## Instructions:

1. In a large bowl, start with the foundation of 1 cup of friendship. This forms the base of your happiness recipe, providing the essential connections that enrich your life.

2. Gently add 2 cups of care, pouring in each measure with tenderness and consideration. Care is the key ingredient that nurtures the soul.

3.  Stir in 2 cups of love, mixing with intention and sincerity. Love infuses every aspect of this recipe with its remarkable flavor.

4.  Slowly incorporate 1 cup of understanding, creating a harmonious blend that fosters empathy and connection.

5.  Sprinkle 1 cup of good thoughts towards others, allowing positivity to permeate the mix and enrich the overall taste.

6.  Add 1 tablespoon of help, acknowledging the importance of lending a hand and supporting those around you.

7.  Generously pour in 2 tablespoons of generosity, a gesture that elevates the essence of giving and sharing.

8.  Fold in 3 tablespoons of laughter, allowing its joyful resonance to infuse every part of the recipe.

9.  Carefully measure 1 teaspoon of happy memories, adding a touch of nostalgia that brings a sense of warmth to the mix.

10. Incorporate 2 teaspoons of smiles, each one a delightful contribution that enhances the final result.

11. Finally, add a pinch of hope, reminding yourself that positivity and optimism are essential elements in this recipe.

12. Gently mix all the ingredients together, ensuring that they blend harmoniously to create a well-rounded and flavorful mixture.

13. Serve this happiness recipe every day, savoring its essence and sharing its joy with those around you.

Note: This recipe is best enjoyed in the company of loved ones, as it encourages the spirit of togetherness and shared happiness. Feel free to customize the proportions and ingredients according to your own preferences, as happiness is a journey unique to everyone.

Why did the bread apply for a job?

Because it wanted to earn some "dough"!

# My Gran's Recipes

## Anne (Gran)

My Mom's Mom.

I am truly fortunate to have a grandmother who is as extraordinary as the one I am blessed with. As I write these words, she is still with us, a remarkable soul who is about to celebrate her ninety-seventh birthday this October. The countless treasured memories of time spent with her have etched a place of honor in my heart, and I am filled with gratitude for the bond we share.

Cooking with my grandmother has been a source of immeasurable joy and warmth. From the simplest tasks, like fetching canned goods from the pantry for our family dinners, to the most festive occasions, her presence has transformed ordinary moments into cherished memories. Birthdays, adorned with laughter and celebration, bear her special touch that makes each one unforgettable.

Our family gatherings, marked by her loving presence, have a magical quality that can only be attributed to her innate ability to create a sense of togetherness and unity. Her love for us is palpable, and it permeates every detail, from the food on the table to the stories shared around it. Each gathering is a testament to her gift of bringing hearts together.

Among the many heartwarming memories, there's a particular triumph that stands out—the day she helped me win first prize in a cake decorating competition. With her guidance and unwavering support, I not only learned the art of cake decorating but also the importance of dedication and creative expression. Her belief in me amplified my confidence, and the victory we achieved together is a testament to her extraordinary influence in my life.

Reflecting on the sum of these experiences, there's no doubt that my grandmother holds a special place in my heart. She embodies love, wisdom, and the essence of what it means to be a nurturing presence in the lives of those she holds dear. Her guidance, her laughter, and her unwavering support have shaped me into the person I am today.

As my grandmother approaches her ninety-seventh birthday, I am reminded of the preciousness of time and the legacy she continues to create. Her spirit remains a beacon of love and inspiration, illuminating the path ahead. With each passing year, she reaffirms the boundless impact one soul can have on those fortunate enough to share in her journey. Indeed, my grandmother is the epitome of the best kind of magic—one that resides in the moments shared and the love felt, forever etching her legacy in the tapestry of our lives.

My grandmother possesses a unique talent that has left a lasting imprint on our family's culinary tradition—her mastery of bread-making. Her hands work their magic with flour, yeast, and a touch of love, transforming simple ingredients into loaves of pure delight. The aroma of freshly baked bread that fills her kitchen is a fragrance of comfort and connection, a reminder of the profound bond we share.

But her culinary prowess extends beyond bread. It's as if she possesses an enchanting ability to conjure a meal fit for an army, even when it seems like there's nothing on hand. Her creativity knows no bounds; she effortlessly transforms humble ingredients into feasts that satisfy both the palate and the heart. It's a skill that defies logic, turning scarcity into abundance and proving that with a dash of ingenuity, anything is possible.

Witnessing her in action is a true marvel. Her hands move with grace, turning a handful of this and a pinch of that into a sumptuous spread that nourishes not just our bodies but also our spirits. Her resourcefulness is a testament to her years of experience and her innate ability to infuse every dish with love and care.

Through her bread-making and culinary wizardry, my grandmother imparts a profound lesson—an embodiment of the notion that cooking isn't merely a task; it's an art form. It's a way to express affection, create memories, and bring people together. Her kitchen is a canvas where ingredients transform into masterpieces, and her heart is the guiding force that infuses every bite with love.

As I look back on the moments spent watching her work her magic, I'm reminded that her skills go beyond the recipes themselves. They're a reflection of her character—her resilience, her adaptability, and her limitless capacity for giving. Her bread and her ability to whip up a meal from seemingly nothing serve as metaphors for the way she approaches life—with a spirit of abundance, generosity, and unwavering love.

My grandmother's hands have created more than meals; they've woven a legacy that's a testament to the beauty of simplicity, the power of resourcefulness, and the magic of sharing food made with love. With each slice of her bread and every plate she sets before us, she reminds us that the greatest feasts are those that nurture not just our bodies but our souls as well.

# Mmmm Gran's Delicious Bread

## Ingredients:

Dry Ingredients:

- 2 cups flour (can be white, whole wheat, or a mix)
- 2 tablespoons quick-rise yeast (place to one side of the bowl)
- 1 teaspoon salt (***keep away from the yeast)
- 3 tablespoons white sugar
- *2-3 more cups of flour (save for later)*

Wet Ingredients:

- 3 tablespoons butter
- 1 cup warm milk (not too hot)
- 1 cup warm water (for bread only; *if making BUNS, use 2 cups of milk—no water—and add 2 eggs)*

## Instructions:

Using a Stand Mixer Machine:

1. In a separate bowl, begin by melting the butter, then add the warm milk and warm water. The liquid should feel warm to the touch but not too hot.
2. In the mixing bowl of your stand mixer, combine these dry ingredients: 2 cups of flour, quick-rise yeast (placed to one

side of the bowl), salt (kept away from yeast), and white sugar.

3.  Slowly pour the warm liquid mixture (butter, milk, and water) into the dry ingredients in the mixing bowl.
4.  Mix for a few moments, then switch to the dough hook attachment and mix at a medium speed for about 3 minutes.
5.  Gradually add the remaining 2-3 cups of flour LITTLE by LITTLE while the mixer is running. Continue to mix until the dough no longer sticks to the sides or bottom of the bowl and has a texture that's not sticky. The total amount of flour may vary, but the goal is to achieve the right texture for fluffy bread.
6.  After adding enough flour, continue to mix for another 2-3 minutes until the dough is well-blended and smooth.

By Hand:

1.  Start by melting the butter, then add the warm milk and warm water. The liquid should feel warm to the touch but not too hot.
2.  In a large mixing bowl, combine the dry ingredients: 2 cups of flour, quick-rise yeast (placed to one side of the bowl), salt (kept away from yeast), and white sugar.
3.  Slowly pour the warm liquid mixture (butter, milk, and water) into the dry ingredients in the bowl. Mix well.
4.  Knead the dough on a lightly floured countertop. Add the remaining 2-3 cups of flour little by little while kneading until the dough reaches a non-sticky texture. This may require up to 3 cups of flour.
5.  Continue kneading for a few more minutes until the dough is smooth and not sticky.

For Both Methods:

1.  If you plan to add seeds or fruit to your bread, do so now and blend them into the dough by hand.
2.  Lightly spread a little butter on a countertop and place the dough on it.
3.  Roll and knead the dough into a mound.
4.  Cover the dough with a clean tea towel and let it rise for about 1 hour or until it doubles in size.

5.  After rising, cut the dough into two halves for loaves of bread...
    or roll it long and cut into smaller pieces for buns.
6.  Knead the dough pieces again and shape them appropriately for the pan you plan to use.
7.  Place the shaped dough into pans
    or on lightly buttered cookie sheets for buns.
8.  Spread a bit of butter on top of the dough.
9.  Cover and let the dough rise again until it doubles in size, approximately ¾ hour to 1 hour.
10. After dough has risen a second time, preheat your oven to 375°F (190°C).
11. Bake the bread in the preheated oven for about 18 minutes, or until the top is golden brown.
    or buns in the preheated oven for about 10+ minutes, or until the top is golden brown.
12. Enjoy your freshly baked Anne's Famous Bread and Buns!

Note: This bread recipe has been handed down through generations and offers the delightful experience of homemade, fresh-baked bread. Whether you make loaves or buns, the result is a delicious, aromatic bread that's perfect for any occasion.

**FOR DIABETICS:** remember that carbs turn into sugar, so if you are going to eat bread use whole wheat flour. Or better yet, try the *Cauliflower Cheese Breadsticks*!

# Crazy Chocolate Cake

## Ingredients:

- 1 cup sugar
- 1 egg
- ½ cup milk
- ½ cup margarine (or butter)
- ¼ teaspoon salt
- 1 teaspoon baking soda
- 1 teaspoon baking powder
- 1 teaspoon vanilla extract
- 1 ½ cups all-purpose flour
- ½ cup cocoa powder
- ½ cup boiling water

## Instructions:

Preheat your oven to 350°F (175°C). Grease and flour an 8x8-inch or 9x9-inch baking pan.

In a large mixing bowl, combine the sugar, egg, milk, margarine (or butter), and vanilla extract. Mix well until the ingredients are fully combined.

In a separate bowl, sift together the flour, cocoa powder, baking soda, baking powder, and salt.

Gradually add the dry ingredients to the wet ingredients, mixing until the batter is smooth.

Carefully stir in the boiling water. The batter will be thin, but that's normal.

Pour the batter into the prepared baking pan.

Bake in the preheated oven for approximately 30 minutes or until a toothpick inserted into the center of the cake comes out clean.

Remove the cake from the oven and allow it to cool in the pan for a few minutes before transferring it to a wire rack to cool completely.

Once the cake is completely cooled, you can frost it with your choice of icing or enjoy it as is.

This Crazy Chocolate Cake is known for its simplicity and great chocolate flavor. It's a perfect dessert for any occasion, and you can customize it with various icings, such as the Chocolate Icing recipe I provided earlier. Enjoy!

## Chocolate Icing

### Ingredients:

- ½ cup unsalted butter
- ⅔ cup cocoa powder
- 3 cups icing sugar (powdered sugar)
- ⅓ cup milk
- 1 teaspoon vanilla extract

### Instructions:

1. In a saucepan or microwave-safe bowl, melt the unsalted butter over low heat or in the microwave until it's completely melted.
2. Stir in the cocoa powder and mix until it forms a smooth paste.
3. Remove the saucepan from the heat (or, if using the microwave, transfer the mixture to a larger mixing bowl).
4. Gradually add the icing sugar and milk alternately, beginning and ending with the icing sugar. Stir well after each addition until the icing is smooth and has a spreading consistency.
5. Stir in the vanilla extract to enhance the flavor of the icing.

6. If the icing is too thick, you can add a little more milk, a tablespoon at a time, until it reaches your desired consistency. If it's too thin, you can add more icing sugar.
7. Once the Crazy Chocolate Cake has cooled completely, spread the Chocolate Icing evenly over the top.
8. Slice and serve your delicious Crazy Chocolate Cake with the rich chocolate icing.

This icing pairs perfectly with the Crazy Chocolate Cake, creating a delightful and decadent chocolate dessert that everyone will enjoy!

**FOR DIABETICS:** not suggested.

# Fancy Icing

## Ingredients:

- 1 cup (2 sticks) butter, softened
- Flavor extract of your choice (e.g., vanilla, almond, lemon), to taste
- Pinch of salt
- 1 tablespoon corn syrup
- 5 ounces (approximately 2/3 cup) milk, added gradually
- 5 cups icing sugar (powdered sugar)
- Food coloring (optional)

## Instructions:

1. In a mixing bowl, whip the softened butter until it's smooth and creamy.
2. Add your choice of flavor extract (e.g., vanilla, almond, lemon) to the butter and mix it in. The amount of extract will depend on your personal preference, so start with a teaspoon and adjust to taste.
3. Add a pinch of salt to enhance the flavor.
4. Stir in the corn syrup. This helps give the icing a smooth and glossy finish.
5. Gradually add the milk, mixing as you pour it in. Continue to mix until the ingredients are well combined, and the mixture is smooth.
6. Begin adding the icing sugar, one cup at a time, beating well after each addition. Keep adding and mixing until you've incorporated all 5 cups of icing sugar.
7. If you want to add color to the icing, you can mix in food coloring, a few drops at a time, until you achieve the desired color.
8. Beat the icing until it's fluffy and smooth. If it's too thick, you can add a little more milk, a tablespoon at a time, to reach your desired consistency. If it's too thin, you can add more icing sugar.
9. Once your Fancy Icing is ready, use it to frost your wedding cake or, gingerbread cake, or any other baked goods that could use a delicious, sweet topping.

This icing is perfect for special occasions and can be customized with various flavor extracts and colors to suit your needs. Enjoy!

**FOR DIABETICS:** not suggested.

# Angel Food Cake Icing

## Ingredients:

- 1 1/2 cups cold milk
- 1 package instant vanilla (or your favorite flavor) pudding mix
- 1 package Dream Whip topping mix (you can usually find this in the baking aisle)

## Instructions:

1. In a mixing bowl, combine the instant vanilla pudding mix and cold milk.
2. Use an electric mixer on low speed to beat the pudding mix and milk together until it's well combined and starts to thicken. This usually takes about 2 minutes.
3. Add the package of Dream Whip topping mix to the pudding mixture.
4. Continue to beat the mixture at high speed until it becomes light and fluffy. This can take around 4-5 minutes.
5. Once the icing is light and fluffy, it's ready to use.
6. You can spread this icing on your angel food cake, cupcakes, or any other desserts you like.

This icing will give your angel food cake a deliciously creamy and light topping.

**FOR DIABETICS:**
not suggested.

# Jumbo Raisin Cookies

## Ingredients:

For the Raisin Mixture:

- 2 cups raisins
- 1 cup water

For the Cookie Dough:

- 1 cup (2 sticks) unsalted butter
- 2 cups granulated sugar
- 3 large eggs
- 1 teaspoon vanilla extract
- Cooked raisin mixture (from above)

For the Dry Ingredients:

- 4 cups all-purpose flour
- 1 teaspoon baking powder
- 1 teaspoon salt
- 1 ½ teaspoons ground cinnamon
- ¼ teaspoon ground nutmeg
- ¼ teaspoon ground allspice

Optional Additions:

- 1 cup chopped nuts (if desired)

## Instructions:

1. Preheat your oven to 375°F (190°C). Line baking sheets with parchment paper or lightly grease them.
2. In a medium-sized saucepan, combine the raisins and water. Bring the mixture to a boil, then reduce the heat and let it simmer for about 5 minutes. Alternatively, you can microwave them for about 2 minutes. Remove from heat and let it cool.
3. In a large mixing bowl, cream together the softened butter and granulated sugar until light and fluffy.

4. Add the eggs, one at a time, beating well after each addition. Stir in the vanilla extract.
5. Pour the cooked raisin mixture (raisins and liquid) into the bowl with the creamed butter and sugar. Mix until well combined.
6. In a separate bowl, whisk together the flour, baking powder, salt, cinnamon, nutmeg, and allspice.
7. Gradually add the dry ingredients to the wet ingredients, mixing until just combined. If desired, stir in the chopped nuts.
8. Drop spoonfuls of cookie dough onto the prepared baking sheets, leaving some space between each cookie.
9. Bake in the preheated oven for 12 to 15 minutes or until the cookies are golden brown around the edges.
10. Remove the cookies from the oven and allow them to cool on the baking sheets for a few minutes before transferring them to wire racks to cool completely.

Enjoy your Jumbo Raisin Cookies with a cup of tea or coffee!

**FOR DIABETICS:** not suggested.

# Fudgesicles

## Ingredients:

- 1 package of instant chocolate pudding mix
- 1/2 cup sugar
- 1/2 cup heavy cream and 2 cups milk
- or 2 1/2 cups of Creamo (a dairy-based creamer)

## Instructions:

1. In a mixing bowl, combine the instant chocolate pudding mix and sugar.
2. Pour in the heavy cream and milk (or Creamo).
3. Stir the mixture vigorously until the pudding mix and sugar are completely dissolved and the mixture is smooth and creamy.
4. Once the mixture is well combined, pour it into your Fudgesicle molds. If you don't have molds, you can use ice cube trays, small paper cups, or any other suitable freezer-safe containers.
5. Insert popsicle sticks, or wooden craft sticks into each mold or cup. Make sure they stand upright.
6. Place the molds or cups in the freezer and let them freeze for several hours or until the Fudgesicles are solid.
7. Once they are frozen, remove the Fudgesicles from the molds or cups. You can dip the molds briefly in warm water to make them easier to remove.
8. Enjoy your homemade Fudgesicles! These creamy chocolate treats are perfect for a cool and refreshing dessert.

Feel free to adjust the sugar amount to suit your sweetness preference. Enjoy your delicious homemade Fudgesicles!

**FOR DIABETICS:** not suggested.

# Tartar Sauce

## Ingredients:

- 1/2 cup mayonnaise
- 1 tablespoon minced fresh dill
- 1 tablespoon sweet green relish
- 2 tablespoons horseradish
- 2 tablespoons lemon juice

## Instructions:

1. In a mixing bowl, combine the mayonnaise, minced fresh dill, sweet green relish, horseradish, and lemon juice.
2. Stir the ingredients together until well-mixed.
3. Taste the tartar sauce and adjust the seasoning to your preference. You can add more lemon juice for acidity, more horseradish for heat, or more relish for sweetness.
4. Once you're satisfied with the flavor, cover the bowl and refrigerate the tartar sauce for at least 30 minutes to allow the flavors to meld together.
5. Serve your homemade tartar sauce as a delicious accompaniment to seafood dishes, such as fish and chips, crab cakes, or fried shrimp.
6. Enjoy your homemade tartar sauce with your favorite seafood!

**FOR DIABETICS:** enjoy!

How do you make holy water?

You boil the hell out of it!

# My Grandma's Recipes

## Jessie (Grandma Fletcher)

My Dad's Mom.

The pages of my family's history are adorned with the exquisite flavors and traditions lovingly preserved by my dad's mother—my grandma. Stepping into her world was like entering a realm of enchantment, where her culinary magic transformed even the simplest occasions into elegant soirées that left an indelible mark on my upbringing.

With her English heritage as a guiding light, my grandma orchestrated dinner parties in her tiny studio room that were nothing short of captivating. The space transformed into a haven of refinement, adorned with polished silverware and delicate crystal glasses that sparkled in the soft glow of candlelight. As I sat at her table, I absorbed not just the flavors but the grace and poise she exuded—an embodiment of etiquette and elegance.

She had a way of making even the simplest ingredients shine with sophistication. Her secret to elevating carrots into a culinary masterpiece was a whisper of brown sugar—a touch that added a hint of sweetness and warmth. It was a secret she entrusted to me with a conspiratorial wink, a shared knowledge that bound us together.

The flavors of her dishes held a special place in my heart, and none more so than her chicken. Years later, the truth emerged—it wasn't chicken but rabbit that lent that distinct taste to her creation. The revelation added layers of depth to my memories, showing how the flavors I cherished were intertwined with tales of ingenuity and resourcefulness.

Yet, amidst all her culinary wonders, the true pinnacle of my visits to Grandma's house was the ice cream. Never had ice cream tasted as exquisite as it did in her presence. The simple act of enjoying a scoop was transformed into an art form—an experience that unfolded with warmed cherry pie filling cascading over the velvety ice cream, creating a symphony of flavors that danced on the taste buds.

The magic of my grandma's recipes was more than the sum of their ingredients. It was a testament to her love, her dedication to creating memories, and her knack for infusing every dish with a touch of elegance. Her legacy continues to inspire me, a reminder that cooking is an art that transcends generations, weaving stories that intertwine flavors and traditions.

As I reflect on the moments shared at her table, I am reminded that her recipes are more than culinary creations—they are vessels of her spirit, carriers of her love. With each bite of a dish crafted in her memory, I taste not just the flavors but the essence of her presence, and I'm transported back to a time of elegance, warmth, and the magic that only a grandmother's touch can conjure.

# Cherry Ice Cream

## Ingredients:

- Vanilla ice cream (store-bought or homemade)
- Cherry pie filling

## Instructions:

1. Allow the vanilla ice cream to soften slightly by leaving it out at room temperature for a few minutes. This will make it easier to scoop and mix.
2. In a separate saucepan, heat the cherry pie filling over low to medium heat on the stove. You can heat it until it's warm or even slightly simmering if you prefer a warm topping, but it's also delicious when served cold over the ice cream.
3. Scoop the softened vanilla ice cream into serving bowls or dishes.
4. Drizzle the warm or room-temperature cherry pie filling over the ice cream. You can adjust the amount of pie filling according to your preference.
5. Serve the Cherry Ice Cream immediately and enjoy the combination of creamy vanilla ice cream with the sweet and fruity cherry topping.

This dessert is perfect for a quick and tasty treat on a warm day or whenever you're in the mood for something sweet and fruity.

**FOR DIABETICS:** not suggested.

# Unbaked Oatmeal Cookies

## Ingredients:

- 2 cups granulated sugar
- ½ cup butter
- ½ cup milk
- 3 cups old-fashioned rolled oats
- ½ cup unsweetened cocoa powder
- 1 cup shredded coconut
- 1 teaspoon vanilla extract
- ½ teaspoon salt

## Instructions:

1. In a large saucepan, combine the sugar, butter, and milk. Bring the mixture to a boil over medium heat, stirring constantly.
2. Once the mixture reaches a rolling boil, continue to boil for exactly 5 minutes, stirring continuously.
3. After 5 minutes, remove the saucepan from heat.
4. Stir in the old-fashioned rolled oats, unsweetened cocoa powder, shredded coconut, vanilla extract, and salt. Mix until all the ingredients are well combined.
5. Line a cookie sheet with parchment paper.
6. Drop spoonfuls of the mixture onto the parchment paper to form individual cookies. You can use a regular spoon or a cookie scoop for this.
7. Allow the cookies to cool and set at room temperature. This will take some time, but they will firm up as they cool.
8. Once the cookies have completely cooled and set, you can enjoy them!

These Unbaked Oatmeal Cookies are a classic no-bake treat with a delightful combination of chocolate, oats, and coconut. Enjoy!

**FOR DIABETICS**: use a sugar substitute.

# Chicken Topping

## Ingredients:

- Parsley flakes
- Celery flakes
- Breadcrumbs
- Poultry seasoning
- Salt and pepper (to taste)
- Melted butter (for brushing on the chicken)

## Instructions:

1. Preheat your oven to 350 degrees Fahrenheit (175 degrees Celsius).
2. Prepare your chicken pieces by cleaning and patting them dry with paper towels. You can use chicken breasts, thighs, drumsticks, or any other preferred cuts.
3. In a bowl, combine the parsley flakes, celery flakes, breadcrumbs, poultry seasoning, and salt and pepper to taste. The quantities of each ingredient can vary depending on your preference, but you can start with roughly equal amounts of parsley flakes, celery flakes, and breadcrumbs and then add poultry seasoning, salt, and pepper to taste.
4. Brush a little melted butter onto the chicken pieces. This will help the seasoning mixture adhere to the chicken and add flavor.
5. Sprinkle the seasoned mixture evenly over the chicken pieces, pressing it down gently to adhere.
6. Place the seasoned chicken in a baking dish or on a baking sheet.
7. Bake in the preheated oven for approximately 60 minutes or until the chicken is cooked through and the topping is golden brown and crispy.
8. Remove the chicken from the oven, let it rest for a few minutes, and then serve.

Adjust the seasoning quantities to suit your taste preferences. Enjoy your meal!

**FOR DIABETICS:** switch breadcrumbs with whole oak flakes!

# Rabbit

## Ingredients:

- 1 whole rabbit, about 3-4 pounds, cleaned and dressed
- 4-5 cloves garlic, minced
- 2-3 sprigs of fresh rosemary or thyme (or 1-2 teaspoons dried)
- 2-3 tablespoons olive oil
- Salt and black pepper, to taste
- 1 lemon, thinly sliced (optional)
- 1 onion, chopped (optional)
- 2-3 cups chicken or vegetable broth (for basting)

## Instructions:

1. Preheat your oven to 350°F (175°C).
2. In a small bowl, combine the minced garlic, rosemary or thyme, olive oil, salt, and black pepper. This will create a flavorful marinade for the rabbit.
3. Rub the rabbit inside and out with the garlic and herb mixture. Make sure to coat it evenly.
4. If desired, stuff the rabbit cavity with lemon slices and chopped onions for extra flavor.
5. Place the rabbit in a roasting pan or on a baking sheet with a rack to allow air to circulate around it.

6. Pour a cup or two of chicken or vegetable broth into the bottom of the roasting pan. This will help keep the rabbit moist while it roasts.
7. Cover the rabbit loosely with aluminum foil. This will help prevent the meat from drying out during the initial roasting.
8. Roast the rabbit in the preheated oven for about 1 hour. After the first 30 minutes, remove the foil and baste the rabbit with the pan juices every 15-20 minutes.
9. Continue roasting until the rabbit's internal temperature reaches 160-165°F (71-74°C) and the skin is golden brown and crispy. The total cooking time will vary depending on the size of the rabbit but is typically around 1.5 to 2 hours.
10. Once the rabbit is cooked, remove it from the oven and let it rest for a few minutes before carving.
11. Carve the rabbit into serving pieces and serve with your choice of side dishes, such as roasted vegetables, mashed potatoes, or a fresh salad.

Enjoy your roasted rabbit with your favorite accompaniments! It's a unique and flavorful dish that's sure to impress your guests.

**FOR DIABETICS:** enjoy!

Why did the cookie go to the
doctor?

Because it was
feeling crumby!

# My Mom's Recipes

## Linda (Nan)

In the heart of our family, my mother stood as a shining example of resilience, creativity, and unwavering love. As a single mother, she possessed a remarkable gift—the ability to transform even the simplest of meals into gourmet delights. Her touch elevated hot dogs to a realm of flavors that danced on our tongues, a testament to her culinary magic.

One scent that lingers in my memory is the aroma of her hobo bread, baked in tins that once held canned goods. The fragrance wafted through our home, carrying with it a sense of comfort and nostalgia. It was a reminder that even with limited resources, my mother's ingenuity could create nourishment that was both satisfying and heartwarming.

Our family's culinary journey was anchored in the classic trio of meat, potatoes, and vegetables. It was a meal that reflected the simplicity and substance of our lives, a reflection of my mother's dedication to providing us with hearty sustenance and a taste of home.

From the delight of roasting marshmallows over an open fire during camping trips to the sizzle of barbecue in our own backyard, our home was a haven of love and family. Each gathering, each meal shared, was an expression of the bonds that tied us together, a testament to the memories we created and the moments we cherished.

My mother, a working mom who juggled responsibilities with grace, had an essential lesson to impart—she believed in teaching us kids how to cook. Her care extended beyond the present moment, instilling in us the invaluable skill of nourishing ourselves and others. Her legacy transcended her own kitchen, reaching into our lives as we embraced her teachings and carried her love for cooking into our own culinary adventures.

As I reflect on those days, I'm reminded that my mother's influence extended far beyond the stove. She taught us that cooking isn't just about food; it's about love, creativity, and the joy of sharing. Her ability to turn mealtimes into celebrations of family and togetherness is a gift that continues to shape our lives.

In the tapestry of my memories, my mother's kitchen is a sacred space—a place where flavors mingle, laughter flows, and bonds grow stronger. Her hot dogs that tasted like gourmet creations and her hobo bread baked with love are more than just dishes; they're threads that weave together the story of a single mom's devotion and the lasting impact of a family united by the simple joys of food and love.

# Gourmet Wieners

## Ingredients:

- Wieners (hot dogs), cut in half lengthwise
- 3/4 cup barbecue sauce
- 3/4 cup ketchup
- 1 tablespoon Worcestershire sauce
- 1/3 cup brown sugar
- 1 can of tomato soup
- Salt, pepper, and garlic powder (to taste)

## Instructions:

1. Preheat your oven to 350 degrees Fahrenheit (175 degrees Celsius).
2. Cut the wieners (hot dogs) in half lengthwise so they are split but not completely separated.
3. In a mixing bowl, combine the barbecue sauce, ketchup, Worcestershire sauce, brown sugar, and a can of tomato soup. Mix these ingredients until well combined.
4. Season the sauce mixture with salt, pepper, and garlic powder to taste. Adjust the seasonings based on your preference for flavor.
5. Place the halved wieners on a baking sheet, arranging them in a single layer.
6. Pour the sauce mixture evenly over the wieners, ensuring they are well coated.
7. Bake in the preheated oven for 15 to 30 minutes or until the wieners are heated through, and the sauce has thickened and caramelized slightly. The exact baking time may vary, so keep an eye on them to prevent burning.
8. Once done, remove the Gourmet Wieners from the oven and let them cool slightly before serving.

These Gourmet Wieners make a tasty and tangy dish that's perfect for parties or a quick weeknight dinner. Enjoy!

**FOR DIABETICS:** use an alternate sugar.

# Hobo Bread

Hobo Bread is a delightful and sweet bread recipe that's baked in cans for a unique presentation. Here's a breakdown of the ingredients and instructions:

## Ingredients:

- 1 1/2 cups hot water
- 3 3/4 cups raisins
- 4 teaspoons baking soda
- 4 tablespoons butter
- 1 1/2 cups brown sugar
- 1 1/2 cups white sugar
- 2 teaspoons vanilla extract
- 1/2 teaspoon salt
- 4 cups all-purpose flour
- 2 large eggs

## Instructions:

1. Preheat your oven to 350 degrees Fahrenheit (175 degrees Celsius).
2. In a large bowl, pour 1 1/2 cups of hot water over the 3 3/4 cups of raisins. Stir in the 4 teaspoons of baking soda. Mix well to ensure the baking soda is dissolved.
3. Add the 4 tablespoons of butter to the raisin mixture. Stir until the butter melts and is well incorporated.
4. Stir in both the 1 1/2 cups of brown sugar and the 1 1/2 cups of white sugar. Mix until the sugars are fully dissolved.
5. Add the 2 teaspoons of vanilla extract and 1/2 teaspoon of salt to the mixture. Stir to combine.
6. Gradually add the 4 cups of all-purpose flour to the mixture. Mix well to form a thick, batter-like consistency.
7. Beat in the 2 large eggs until they are fully incorporated into the batter.
8. Prepare 7 clean 15 oz cans by greasing them well and removing any labels. Make sure the cans are dry.

9. Divide the batter evenly among the greased cans, filling each can about two-thirds full.

10. Place the filled cans on a baking sheet or rack and bake in the preheated oven for 45 to 60 minutes or until a toothpick or skewer inserted into the center of the bread comes out clean.

11. Once done, remove the cans from the oven and allow them to cool slightly. To cool, invert the cans upside down on a wire rack to release the bread from the cans. Be careful as the cans may still be hot.

12. Once completely cooled, you can remove the bread from the cans by gently tapping the open end on a countertop.

Hobo Bread is a unique and delicious treat that's great for sharing with friends and family. Enjoy!

**FOR DIABETICS:** not suggested.

# Sour Dough Appetizer

Savory Spinach and Seafood Dip in Sourdough Bowl

## Ingredients:

- 1 Round Sour Dough Bread, hollowed out (save bread and tear into pieces)
- 1 small container of sour cream
- 1 large container of plain yogurt
- Vegetable soup mix, to taste
- Fresh Spinach, torn up
- 1 can of drained shrimp or crab

## Instructions:

1. Begin by hollowing out the Round Sour Dough Bread, creating a bowl-like shape. Save the removed bread and tear it into bite-sized pieces to serve as dippers later.
2. In a mixing bowl, combine the small container of sour cream and the large container of plain yogurt. These creamy bases will form the foundation of your dip.
3. Gradually add the vegetable soup mix to the creamy mixture, adjusting the amount to your taste preferences. The soup mix will infuse the dip with savory flavors, so you can start with a small amount and adjust as needed.
4. Gently fold in the torn fresh spinach, allowing its vibrant color and earthy taste to add a delightful dimension to the dip.
5. Carefully drain the can of shrimp or crab and add it to the mixture. These seafood elements will bring a touch of oceanic goodness to the dip.
6. Stir the mixture thoroughly, ensuring that all the ingredients are well combined and the flavors are evenly distributed.
7. Allow the mixture to sit for about an hour, letting the flavors meld together and create a harmonious blend.
8. Once the dip has had time to infuse, spoon the mixture into the hollowed-out sourdough bread bowl. Spread it evenly to ensure each scoop offers a perfect balance of flavors.

9. Place the reserved torn bread pieces around the bread bowl on the serving plate. These bread pieces will serve as delectable dippers that perfectly complement the savory dip.
10. Present your Savory Spinach and Seafood Dip in Sourdough Bowl to your guests, inviting them to savor the delightful blend of creamy textures, savory notes, and oceanic accents.
11. Encourage your guests to dip the torn bread pieces into the creamy mixture, creating a culinary experience that combines the goodness of the dip with the satisfying crunch of the bread.

Note: This recipe is a celebration of flavors and textures, offering a delightful combination of creamy, savory, and oceanic elements. The hollowed-out sourdough bread bowl not only serves as a vessel for the dip but also provides an edible component that enhances the overall experience. Whether enjoyed as an appetizer or a gathering centerpiece, this dip offers a blend of tastes that will tantalize the palate and leave guests asking for more.

**FOR DIABETICS:** enjoy dipping nut/seed crackers or fresh vegies into the dip.

# Homemade BBQ Sauce with a Touch of Smoke

Ingredients:

- ½ minced onion
- 1 clove garlic, minced
- 3 tablespoons butter
- 1 cup ketchup
- ¼ cup vinegar
- 2 tablespoons brown sugar
- 2 teaspoons mustard
- 2 tablespoons Worcestershire sauce
- Salt and pepper, to taste
- 5-10 drops of liquid smoke

Instructions:

1. Begin by sautéing the minced onion, minced garlic, and butter in a saucepan over medium heat. Allow the onion and garlic to become fragrant and tender while the butter lends its richness to the base of the sauce.
2. Once the onion and garlic are sautéed to perfection, add the ketchup, vinegar, and brown sugar to the saucepan. These ingredients will form the core of your BBQ sauce, providing a balance of tanginess and sweetness.
3. Incorporate the mustard and Worcestershire sauce into the mixture, adding layers of depth and flavor to your homemade BBQ sauce.
4. Season the sauce with salt and pepper according to your taste preferences. The seasonings will enhance the overall taste and help create a well-rounded flavor profile.
5. Introduce 5-10 drops of liquid smoke to the sauce. Liquid smoke is a concentrated flavor that imparts a smoky essence to your BBQ sauce, reminiscent of traditional smoky barbecue flavors.
6. Stir the mixture well to ensure all the ingredients are thoroughly combined and the flavors meld together.

7. Reduce the heat to low and allow the sauce to simmer gently for about 20 minutes. This simmering process will help the flavors meld, intensify, and create a rich and aromatic BBQ sauce.

8. As the sauce simmers, take a moment to appreciate the aroma that fills your kitchen—a harmonious blend of onion, garlic, tanginess, sweetness, and the delightful smokiness.

9. After 20 minutes, your Homemade BBQ Sauce with a Touch of Smoke is ready. The flavors have developed beautifully, creating a sauce that captures the essence of traditional barbecue.

10. Remove the saucepan from the heat and let the sauce cool slightly before transferring it to a storage container or serving dish.

11. Your homemade BBQ sauce is now ready to be enjoyed. Use it to marinate, baste, or dip your favorite grilled or smoked dishes, adding a layer of homemade goodness to your barbecue creations.

12. Store in in fridge.

Note: This homemade BBQ sauce combines the convenience of store-bought sauce with the satisfaction of crafting your own flavorful blend. The sautéed onion, garlic, and butter set the stage for a sauce that is both rich and inviting. The addition of liquid smoke infuses a touch of smokiness, elevating the sauce to a level that's reminiscent of classic barbecue flavors. Whether enjoyed on ribs, chicken, burgers, or vegetables, this sauce will undoubtedly become a staple in your culinary repertoire.

**FOR DIABETICS:** replace sugar with alternative, and you can buy no-sugar ketchup.

# Honey Mustard Dip

## Ingredients:

- 1/3 cup mayonnaise
- 2 tablespoons Dijon mustard
- 2 tablespoons honey
- 2 teaspoons fresh lemon juice
- Salt and pepper to taste

## Instructions:

1. In a small mixing bowl, combine the mayonnaise, Dijon mustard, honey, and fresh lemon juice.
2. Mix the ingredients together until you have a smooth and well-incorporated dip.
3. Taste the dip and season it with a pinch of salt and a dash of pepper. Adjust the seasoning to your preference, adding more salt or pepper if needed.
4. Once you're satisfied with the flavor and consistency, transfer the honey mustard dip to a serving bowl or container.
5. Serve the dip immediately with your favorite foods. It's perfect for dipping chicken tenders, pretzels, and vegetables or as a sauce for sandwiches and salads.

**FOR DIABETICS:** enjoy!

# Meatballs

## Ingredients:

For the Meatballs:

- 1 pound ground beef (hamburger)
- 1/4 cup breadcrumbs
- 1 egg, beaten
- 1/2 teaspoon garlic salt
- 1/4 teaspoon black pepper

For the Sauce:

- 1/2 cup brown sugar
- 1 tablespoon cornstarch
- 1/3 cup water
- 1/4 cup vinegar
- 1 tablespoon soy sauce
- 1 tablespoon vegetable oil
- 1 onion, diced
- 1 green pepper, diced
- 2 carrots, shredded
- 1 chicken bouillon cube

## Instructions:

For the Meatballs:

1. In a large mixing bowl, combine the ground beef, breadcrumbs, beaten egg, garlic salt, and black pepper. Mix until well combined.
2. Shape the mixture into meatballs, forming them into 1-inch to 1.5-inch balls. You should get approximately 20-24 meatballs, depending on the size.

3. Heat a large skillet or frying pan over medium heat and add a bit of oil if it's not non-stick.
4. Carefully place the meatballs in the hot skillet and cook them, turning occasionally, until they are browned on all sides and cooked through. This should take about 8-10 minutes. Remove the cooked meatballs from the skillet and set them aside.

For the Sauce:

5. In the same skillet, add the diced onion, diced green pepper, and shredded carrots. Sauté the vegetables for about 8 minutes or until they become tender.
6. While the vegetables are cooking, dissolve the chicken bouillon cube in 1/3 cup of water.
7. In a separate bowl, whisk together the brown sugar, cornstarch, vinegar, soy sauce, and vegetable oil.
8. Pour the bouillon mixture and the brown sugar mixture into the skillet with the sautéed vegetables. Stir everything together and cook for a few minutes until the sauce thickens and becomes glossy.

Combining Meatballs and Sauce:

9. Return the cooked meatballs to the skillet with the sauce. Stir them gently to coat the meatballs evenly with the sauce.
10. Allow the meatballs to simmer in the sauce for a few more minutes to heat through and absorb some of the flavors.
11. Once the meatballs are hot and the sauce is well-incorporated, serve them hot over rice or noodles, garnished with chopped green onions or sesame seeds if desired.

**FOR DIABETICS:** use alternative sugar.

# Perfectly Cooked Beans

## Ingredients:

- 1 cup dried beans (e.g., black beans, pinto beans, kidney beans, etc.)
- 3 cups water
- 1 teaspoon salt

## Instructions:

1. Begin by selecting the type of dried beans you'd like to cook. Common varieties include black beans, pinto beans, kidney beans, and more.
2. Measure 1 cup of dried beans and place them in a large bowl. Add 3 cups of water to the bowl, ensuring that the beans are fully submerged.
3. Allow the beans to soak overnight. This soaking process helps rehydrate the beans and reduce their cooking time. The beans will absorb water and expand in size.
4. After the soaking period, drain and rinse the soaked beans thoroughly under cold water. This helps remove any residual impurities and prepares the beans for cooking.
5. Place the rinsed beans in a pot and add 1 teaspoon of salt for each cup of soaked beans. The salt will enhance the flavor of the beans as they cook.
6. Fill the pot with enough water to cover the beans completely. The water-to-bean ratio should be around 3:1 (3 cups of water for every 1 cup of soaked beans).
7. Place the pot on the stove and bring the water to a boil over medium-high heat.
8. Once the water reaches a boil, reduce the heat to low and let the beans simmer. Cover the pot with a lid, leaving a slight opening to allow steam to escape.
9. Allow the beans to simmer gently for about 1.5 to 2 hours. The cooking time can vary depending on the type of beans and their age. Check the beans periodically for tenderness.
10. To check if the beans are done, take a few beans and test their texture. They should be tender but not mushy. Cooking times

may need to be adjusted based on your preference for bean tenderness.

11. Once the beans are cooked to your desired level of tenderness, drain off any excess water.
12. Your perfectly cooked beans are now ready to be enjoyed in a variety of dishes. Use them as a base for soups, stews, and salads or as a flavorful and protein-rich addition to your meals.

Note: Cooking dried beans from scratch allows you to control the level of tenderness and flavor. The soaking process helps rehydrate the beans, reducing their cooking time and ensuring even cooking. With the simple addition of salt, water, and a patient simmer, you'll have a batch of perfectly cooked beans that are versatile and ready to enhance your culinary creations.

**FOR DIABETICS:** enjoy!

# Simple Dumplings for Stew

## Ingredients:

- 2 cups all-purpose flour
- 4 teaspoons baking powder
- ½ teaspoon salt
- 1/3 cup butter
- ¾ cup milk

## Instructions:

1. In a mixing bowl, combine the all-purpose flour, baking powder, and salt. Mix these dry ingredients together until well incorporated.
2. Cut the butter into small pieces and add it to the dry ingredients in the bowl.
3. Use a pastry cutter or fork to blend the butter into the dry ingredients. Continue mixing until the mixture resembles coarse crumbs and the butter is evenly distributed.
4. Gradually pour in the milk while stirring the mixture with a fork. Continue to stir until the dough comes together into a soft and slightly sticky ball. You may need to adjust the amount of milk slightly depending on the consistency of the dough.
5. Once the dough has formed, lightly flour a clean surface.
6. Turn the dough out onto the floured surface and gently knead it a few times to make it smooth. Avoid over-kneading, as this can make the dumplings tough.
7. Roll out the dough to a thickness of about 1/2 inch.
8. Use a knife or cookie cutter to cut the dough into small dumpling shapes or squares.
9. In a pot of simmering stew or soup, carefully place the dumplings on top of the liquid. Make sure they are evenly spaced.
10. Cover the pot with a lid and allow the dumplings to cook for 15-17 minutes. During this time, the dumplings will puff up and become fluffy as they steam and cook in the stew.

11. After the cooking time, the dumplings should be fully cooked, fluffy, and lightly browned on the top.

12. Serve your simple dumplings hot with the stew or soup of your choice. Enjoy their comforting texture and flavor!

These simple dumplings are a wonderful addition to stews and soups, adding a comforting and hearty element to your meals. The basic ingredients and straightforward preparation make them a quick and satisfying choice for any homemade stew.

**FOR DIABETICS:** not suggested.

# Christmas Breakfast Casserole

## Ingredients:

- 16 slices of bread (crusts removed)
- 1 lb shaved cooked ham or sliced ham
- 1 ½ cups grated cheese (your choice, such as cheddar or Swiss)
- 6 eggs
- Salt and pepper to taste
- 1 teaspoon dry mustard
- ¼ cup chopped onion
- 2 teaspoons Worcestershire sauce
- 3 cups milk
- ¼ lb (1/2 cup) butter
- A dash of Tabasco sauce
- Crushed cornflakes or Special K cereal for topping

## Instructions:

1. Start by buttering a 9x13-inch baking dish.
2. Place 8 slices of bread in the bottom of the buttered baking dish, ensuring that the bottom is completely covered.
3. Layer the cooked ham on top of the bread slices, followed by a generous layer of grated cheese.
4. Add the remaining 8 slices of bread on top to create a sandwich-like structure.
5. In a mixing bowl, whisk together the eggs, salt, pepper, dry mustard, chopped onion, Worcestershire sauce, and a dash of Tabasco sauce until well combined.
6. Warm the milk and butter together in a saucepan over medium heat until the butter is melted. Gradually add this mixture to the egg mixture, stirring continuously.
7. Pour the combined egg and milk mixture evenly over the layered bread, ham, and cheese in the baking dish.
8. Cover the baking dish with foil or plastic wrap and refrigerate it overnight to allow the flavors to meld.
9. In the morning, preheat your oven to 350°F (175°C).

CONSTANCE SANTEGO

10. Melt the remaining butter and pour it evenly over the top of the casserole.
11. Sprinkle crushed cornflakes or Special K cereal on top to create a crispy topping.
12. Bake the Christmas Breakfast Casserole, uncovered, for about 1 hour, or until it's golden brown on top and set in the center. The baking time may vary slightly, so keep an eye on it.
13. Once it's done, remove it from the oven and let it cool slightly before serving.

Enjoy this delicious and hearty Christmas Breakfast Casserole with your loved ones during the holiday season. It's a delightful and make-ahead dish that allows you to spend more time celebrating and less time in the kitchen.

This casserole pairs wonderfully with hash browns, bacon, and a festive drink like a Mimosa or your preferred beverage.

*The combination of orange juice and champagne is typically called a "Mimosa." A Mimosa is a popular brunch cocktail made by mixing equal parts of orange juice and champagne or sparkling wine. It's a refreshing and bubbly drink enjoyed in many parts of the world.*

FOR DIABETICS: **Oatmeal flakes** can be a suitable diabetes-friendly alternative to Special K or cornflakes as a topping for your Christmas Breakfast Casserole. Oatmeal is known for its slow-digesting carbohydrates and fiber, which can help stabilize blood sugar levels. Here's how you can use oatmeal flakes as a topping:

### *Instructions:*

1. In place of crushed cornflakes or Special K, use rolled oats or old-fashioned oats. These oats have a hearty texture and provide a pleasant nutty flavor.
2. Sprinkle the rolled oats evenly over the casserole before baking.
3. Bake the casserole as directed in your recipe.
4. When done, the rolled oats will become slightly toasted and add a delightful crunch to the top of your casserole.

Using rolled oats or old-fashioned oats as a topping not only adds a great texture but also introduces the nutritional benefits of oats, such

83

as fiber and complex carbohydrates, which can help manage blood sugar levels. Just ensure that the oats are plain and not the sweetened or flavored varieties to keep the dish diabetes-friendly.

Or

- **Crushed Almonds**: Almonds are a low-carb nut that can add a satisfying crunch to your casserole. Crushed or slivered almonds work well.
- **Chopped Pecans**: Pecans have a sweet and buttery flavor that can enhance the dish. Chop them finely and sprinkle them over the top.
- **Crushed Walnuts**: Walnuts provide a rich and earthy flavor. Crushed walnuts add a nice texture.
- **Sunflower Seeds**: Sunflower seeds are a nutritious and crunchy choice. They are lower in carbohydrates than cereals like Special K.
- **Flaxseed Meal:** Ground flaxseed meal can be used as a topping. It's high in fiber and healthy fats, making it suitable for a diabetes-friendly diet.
- **Chia Seeds:** Chia seeds can add a unique texture and a boost of fiber. They absorb liquid and become gel-like when mixed with the egg and milk mixture.

*Alicia, Nick and DeJounté enjoying Christmas breakfast.*

# Cherry Crisp

## Ingredients:

For the Bottom:

- 3 cups fresh or frozen cherries, pitted
- 3 tablespoons granulated sugar
- 2 tablespoons cornstarch
- ½ tablespoon lemon juice
- ⅛ teaspoon almond extract

For the Top:

- ¾ cup brown sugar
- ½ cup all-purpose flour
- ½ cup granola cereal
- ½ cup (1 stick) unsalted butter, cold and cut into small cubes
- ¾ teaspoon ground cinnamon
- 1 ½ teaspoons ground nutmeg

## Instructions:

1. Preheat your oven to 350°F (175°C). Grease a 9x9-inch baking dish or a similar-sized ovenproof dish.
2. In a large mixing bowl, combine the pitted cherries, granulated sugar, cornstarch, lemon juice, and almond extract. Toss to coat the cherries evenly.
3. Pour the cherry mixture into the prepared baking dish, spreading it out evenly.
4. In a separate mixing bowl, combine the brown sugar, all-purpose flour, granola cereal, cold cubed butter, ground cinnamon, and ground nutmeg.
5. Use a pastry cutter or your fingers to work the butter into the dry ingredients until you have a crumbly topping. This may take a few minutes, but it should resemble coarse crumbs when it's ready.
6. Sprinkle the crumbly topping evenly over the cherry mixture in the baking dish.

7. Place the baking dish in the preheated oven and bake for approximately 30 minutes, or until the topping is golden brown and the cherry filling is bubbling.
8. Remove the Cherry Crisp from the oven and let it cool slightly before serving.
9. Serve warm with a scoop of vanilla ice cream or a dollop of whipped cream, if desired.

Enjoy this warm and comforting Cherry Crisp with its sweet cherry filling and crunchy oat topping—it's the perfect dessert for any occasion!

**FOR DIABETICS:** not suggested.

# Carrot Cake

## Ingredients:

- 4 eggs
- 3 cups raw carrots, grated
- ½ cup of pineapple or grated apple (optional)
- 3 cups all-purpose flour
- 2 teaspoons baking powder
- 2 teaspoons baking soda
- 1 teaspoon vanilla extract
- 1 cup raisins
- 2 cups granulated sugar
- 1 ½ cups vegetable oil
- ¼ teaspoon salt
- ½ cup nuts
  (optional)

## Instructions:

1. Preheat your oven to 350°F (175°C). Grease and flour a 9x13-inch baking pan or two 9-inch round cake pans.
2. In a large mixing bowl, beat together the vegetable oil and granulated sugar until well combined.
3. Add the eggs one at a time, beating well after each addition.
4. Stir in the grated carrots and vanilla extract.
5. In a separate bowl, whisk together the flour, baking powder, baking soda, and salt.
6. Gradually add the dry ingredients to the wet ingredients, mixing until just combined.
7. Fold in the raisins and nuts (if using).
8. Pour the cake batter into the prepared baking pan(s).
9. Bake in the preheated oven for about 40 minutes if using a 9x13-inch pan or 25-30 minutes if using round cake pans. The cake is done when a toothpick inserted into the center comes out clean.

10. Remove the cake from the oven and let it cool in the pan(s) for about 10 minutes before transferring it to a wire rack to cool completely.

## Philadelphia Cream Cheese Icing

### Ingredients:

- 1 (4-ounce) package cream cheese, softened
- ¼ cup unsalted butter, softened
- ½ teaspoon vanilla extract
- 1 cup icing sugar (powdered sugar)

### Instructions:

1. In a mixing bowl, cream together the softened cream cheese and unsalted butter until smooth.
2. Stir in the vanilla extract.
3. Gradually add the icing sugar, beating until the icing is smooth and well combined.
4. Once the cake has cooled completely, spread the Philadelphia Cream Cheese Icing evenly over the top.
5. Slice and serve your delicious homemade Carrot Cake.

Enjoy this classic and moist carrot cake with rich cream cheese icing—it's a delightful dessert that's perfect for any occasion!

**FOR DIABETICS:** not suggested.

# Coleslaw

## Ingredients:

- 4 1/2 cups shredded carrots and cabbage (you can use pre-shredded coleslaw mix)
- 1/2 cup diced onions (you can adjust the amount to your liking)
- 3/4 cup Miracle Whip (or your preferred mayonnaise-based dressing)
- 1 tablespoon sandwich spread (like relish or mustard-based)
- 3/4 tablespoon pickle juice (from your preferred pickles)
- 1 teaspoon salt (adjust to taste)
- 1/4 teaspoon black pepper (adjust to taste)
- 1/3 cup sugar (adjust to taste)
- 4 tablespoons milk

## Instructions:

1. **Prepare the Vegetables:** If you haven't already, shred the carrots and cabbage finely. You can use a food processor or a box grater for this. Dice the onions as well. Combine the shredded vegetables and diced onions in a large mixing bowl.
2. **Prepare the Dressing:** In a separate bowl, whisk together the Miracle Whip (or mayonnaise-based dressing), sandwich spread, pickle juice, salt, pepper, and sugar until the sugar is dissolved. You can adjust the amount of sugar, salt, and pepper to suit your taste.
3. **Thin the Dressing:** Add the milk to the dressing mixture and whisk until well combined. The milk helps to thin the dressing and achieve the desired consistency.
4. **Combine:** Pour the dressing over the shredded vegetables and onions. Stir everything together until the vegetables are evenly coated with the dressing. Make sure the coleslaw is well-mixed.
5. **Chill:** Cover the bowl with plastic wrap or a lid and refrigerate the coleslaw for at least an hour before serving. This allows the flavors to meld together and the coleslaw to chill. You can also refrigerate it longer for even better flavor.

6. **Serve:** Serve your homemade coleslaw as a side dish at barbecues, picnics, alongside sandwiches, or with any meal where coleslaw is a tasty addition.

**FOR DIABETICS:** use alternative sugar.

# Nan's Tartar Sauce

## Ingredients:

- 1/2 cup mayonnaise
- 1 small dill pickle, finely chopped (about 3 tablespoons)
- 1 tablespoon fresh lemon juice
- 1 tablespoon chopped fresh dill (or 1 teaspoon dried dill)
- 1/2 to 1 teaspoon Worcestershire sauce
- 1/2 teaspoon Dijon mustard (optional)
- Salt and pepper to taste

## Instructions:

1. In a mixing bowl, combine 1/2 cup mayonnaise, 3 tablespoons finely chopped dill pickle, 1 tablespoon fresh lemon juice, and 1 tablespoon chopped fresh dill (or 1 teaspoon dried dill).
2. Add 1/2 to 1 teaspoon Worcestershire sauce to the mixture. The amount can be adjusted to your taste. Worcestershire sauce adds depth of flavor, so start with a little and add more if desired.
3. If you prefer a bit of tanginess and extra flavor, add 1/2 teaspoon of Dijon mustard to the mixture. This is optional, but it can enhance the tartar sauce.
4. Season with salt and pepper to taste. Remember, you can always add more salt and pepper later, so start with a small pinch of each.
5. Mix all the ingredients together until creamy and well combined.
6. Taste the tartar sauce and adjust the seasonings if needed. You can add more lemon juice for extra tang, Worcestershire sauce for depth, or dill for a stronger herbal flavor.

7.  Once the tartar sauce reaches your desired taste and consistency, transfer it to a serving dish or an airtight container.
8.  Serve the homemade tartar sauce with your favorite seafood dishes, such as fish and chips, fried shrimp, or crab cakes.

**FOR DIABETICS:** enjoy!

# Thousand Island Dressing

Even the first two ingredients will work 😊

## Ingredients:

- 1/2 cup mayonnaise
- 2 tablespoons ketchup
- 2 tablespoons sweet pickle relish
- 1 tablespoon finely minced onion
- 1 small clove garlic, minced (optional)
- 1 teaspoon white vinegar
- 1 teaspoon white sugar
- 1/2 teaspoon Worcestershire sauce
- Salt and pepper to taste

## Instructions:

1. Combine Ingredients: In a bowl, combine the mayonnaise, ketchup, sweet pickle relish, minced onion, minced garlic (if using), white vinegar, white sugar, and Worcestershire sauce.
2. Mix Thoroughly: Stir all the ingredients together until well combined. Ensure that the sugar is completely dissolved into the mixture.
3. Season: Taste the dressing and adjust the flavor to your liking. Add salt and pepper to taste. Keep in mind that pickle relish can be salty, so you might not need much additional salt.
4. Chill: Refrigerate the Thousand Island dressing for at least 30 minutes before using. Chilling allows the flavors to meld together and enhances the taste.
5. Serve: Use your homemade Thousand Island dressing as a salad dressing, sandwich spread, or dip. It's particularly popular in salads like the classic Reuben salad or as a topping for burgers and sandwiches.
6. Store: Store any leftover dressing in an airtight container in the refrigerator for up to a week.

**FOR DIABETICS:** use alternative sugar.

What did one plate say to
the other plate?

"Lunch is on me!"

# My Mother-In-Law's Recipes

## Marlene (Grammy)

The heart of my husband's family was my mother-in-law. She stood as

a beacon of love, craftsmanship, and culinary delight. Her presence was a familiar comfort, as she often found herself immersed in her two passions— needlepoint and the kitchen, with the latter being her domain of creativity and affection.

Baking was her language of love, a way to communicate her deepest emotions through the medium of desserts. The creations that emerged from her oven were nothing short of wondrous. Each bite carried with it a piece of her heart, a testament to her dedication to nurturing us with flavors that transcended the ordinary.

Among the many treasures she bestowed upon us, her pie crust was a work of art in its own right. Flaky, buttery, and delicate, it cradled the most delectable fillings that transformed each pie into a masterpiece. The love she poured into her pastry was palpable, and with every slice, we tasted her devotion.

Canned pickles were another of her specialties, capturing the essence of summer in each jar. The crunch of the vegetables, the tangy brine—it was as if she had bottled the warmth of the sun and the joy of harvest. Opening a jar of her pickles was like unlocking a treasure chest of memories, a reminder of the love that infused every jar she meticulously prepared.

Cabbage rolls, lovingly assembled, were a symbol of her culinary prowess. Each roll was a labor of love, a fusion of flavors that told a story of tradition and care. With every bite, we tasted not only the ingredients but also the history and heritage she carried within her.

And then there was her fudge—a symphony of sweetness that danced on our tongues. Rich, creamy, and indulgent, her fudge was a testament to the artistry she wielded in the kitchen. It was as if she condensed her love into each square, and with every piece we savored, we felt her affection enveloping us.

As I reflect on the memories of her culinary creations, I am reminded that her love knew no bounds. Her kitchen was a canvas, and every dish was a stroke of passion and devotion. Whether in the midst of her needlepoint or immersed in the alchemy of baking, she left an indelible mark on our lives.

Her desserts were more than just treats; they were vessels of her love, carriers of her legacy. The memories of her pie crust, pickles, cabbage rolls, and fudge are etched in our hearts as a reminder of the precious moments we shared and the enduring love she showered upon us. In every dish she prepared, in every stitch she sewed, she imprinted her spirit on our lives—a testament to the beauty of the art of giving and the lasting impact of a mother-in-law who showed her love through the language of food.

# Dill Pickles

## Ingredients:

- 3 quarts (12 cups) of water
- 1 cup coarse salt
- 3 cups white vinegar
- Fresh cucumbers, cleaned and prepared
- Fresh dill sprigs
- Garlic cloves
- Pickling spices

## Instructions:

1. In a large pot, combine 3 quarts of water and 1 cup of coarse salt. Stir the mixture well to dissolve the salt. This brine solution will be the base for your pickling process.
2. Place the pot on the stove and bring the brine solution to a boil. Allow it to boil for about 2 minutes, ensuring that the salt is fully dissolved.
3. Once the brine has boiled, carefully remove the pot from the heat source. You now have your pickling solution ready to infuse your cucumbers with flavor.
4. Prepare your cucumbers by washing and cleaning them thoroughly. Trim the ends if needed and cut them into slices spears, or leave them whole, depending on your preference.
5. In each sterilized glass jar, place a sprig of fresh dill, a garlic clove, and about ½ teaspoon of pickling spices. These aromatic elements will lend their distinctive flavors to your pickles.
6. Carefully pack the prepared cucumbers into the jars, ensuring they are placed snugly but not overly compressed.
7. Gently pour the prepared brine solution over the cucumbers in each jar. The brine should cover the cucumbers completely, ensuring even pickling.
8. Seal the jars with sterilized lids and rings, ensuring they are closed tightly.
9. Allow the jars to cool to room temperature before transferring them to the refrigerator.

10. Place the sealed jars of cucumbers in the refrigerator and let them sit for about 1 to 2 weeks. During this time, the flavors will meld together, and the cucumbers will transform into delicious dill pickles.
11. As the pickles mature, the flavors will intensify, creating a delightful balance of dill, garlic, and pickling spices.
12. Once your dill pickles have reached your desired level of flavor, they are ready to be enjoyed as a crunchy and tangy treat.

Note: These homemade dill pickles are a testament to the traditional art of pickling. The combination of fresh cucumbers, aromatic dill, garlic, and pickling spices creates a medley of flavors that celebrate the essence of preserving. These pickles are perfect as a condiment, a snack, or a tasty addition to sandwiches and salads. Enjoy the fruits of your pickling labor, and savor the joy of crafting your own delicious dill pickles from scratch.

**FOR DIABETICS:** enjoy!

# Barley and Bacon Hotpot

## Ingredients:

- 1 ½ cups pearl barley
- ½ pound bacon, cut into pieces
- 2 tablespoons butter
- 2 large onions, chopped
- 1 ½ cups sliced carrots
- 1 celery stalk, chopped
- 2 cups thinly sliced mushrooms
- 3 cups chicken broth
- 4 tablespoons chopped parsley
- Salt and pepper to taste

## Instructions:

1. Preheat your oven to 350°F (175°C).
2. In a Dutch oven (or a large, oven-safe pot with a lid), melt the butter over medium heat. If you prefer, you can cook the bacon separately and then add it later.
3. Add the bacon to the Dutch oven and cook for about 5 minutes or until it starts to become crispy.
4. Stir in the chopped onions, carrots, celery, mushrooms, and pearl barley. Cook for a few minutes until the vegetables begin to soften.
5. Pour in the chicken broth and add the chopped parsley. Season with salt and pepper according to your taste.
6. Bring the mixture to a boil while stirring occasionally.
7. Once it reaches a boil, cover the Dutch oven with its lid.
8. Transfer the covered Dutch oven to the preheated oven and bake for approximately 1 hour.
9. Check the casserole after 1 hour. The barley should be soft, and most of the liquid should be absorbed or evaporated. If it needs more time, you can continue baking until the desired consistency is reached.
10. Once done, remove the Dutch oven from the oven and let it sit for a few minutes before serving.
11. Serve your delicious Barley and Bacon Casserole hot as a hearty and comforting dish.

This casserole combines the nutty flavor and chewy texture of pearl barley with the savory goodness of bacon and vegetables. It's a flavorful and satisfying meal perfect for any occasion.

**FOR DIABETICS:** enjoy!

# Scalloped Potatoes

## Ingredients:

- 4 cups thinly sliced potatoes (about 4 medium-sized potatoes)
- 1/4 cup all-purpose flour
- 1/4 cup butter
- 1/2 cup chopped onion
- 1 teaspoon salt
- 1/4 teaspoon black pepper
- 2 cups milk
- 1 1/2 cups shredded cheddar cheese (or cheese of your choice)

## Instructions:

1. Preheat your oven to 350°F (175°C).
2. In a medium saucepan over medium heat, melt the butter.
3. Add the chopped onions to the melted butter and sauté them until they become translucent and fragrant, usually about 3-5 minutes.
4. Stir in the flour, salt, and black pepper to create a roux. Cook the roux for about 1-2 minutes, stirring constantly until it's light golden brown.
5. Gradually add the milk to the roux, whisking continuously to avoid lumps. Cook and stir until the mixture thickens and begins to bubble.
6. Remove the saucepan from the heat.
7. In a greased 2-quart baking dish, layer half of the sliced potatoes.
8. Pour half of the prepared sauce over the potatoes.
9. Repeat with the remaining potatoes and sauce.
10. Cover the baking dish with aluminum foil or a lid and bake in the preheated oven for about 1 1/2 to 2 hours or until the potatoes are tender and the top is golden brown. Check the potatoes with a fork to ensure they are cooked through.
11. About 10-15 minutes before the potatoes are done, remove the cover and sprinkle the shredded cheese evenly over the top.

12. Continue baking, uncovered, until the cheese is melted and bubbly, and the top is nicely browned.
13. Once done, remove the scalloped potatoes from the oven and let them rest for a few minutes before serving.

Enjoy your homemade scalloped potatoes as a delicious and comforting side dish. This recipe combines creamy, cheesy goodness with tender slices of potatoes for a satisfying dish that pairs well with various main courses.

**FOR DIABETICS:** substitute the flour with almond flour.

# Raisin Cake With Fudge Icing

## Ingredients:

- 1 cup raisins
- 1 cup white sugar
- 1 egg
- 1 cup chopped nuts (of your choice)
- 1/2 cup butter
- 2 cups all-purpose flour
- 1/2 teaspoon nutmeg
- 1/2 teaspoon cinnamon
- 1/2 teaspoon baking soda
- 1/2 teaspoon baking powder
- 1 cup reserved water from boiling raisins

## Instructions:

1. Preheat your oven to 350°F (175°C). Grease and flour a 9x9-inch square baking pan.
2. In a saucepan, bring 1 cup of raisins and enough water to cover them to a boil. Boil for 2 minutes, then drain off the water. Save 1 cup of the reserved raisin water for the batter.
3. In a mixing bowl, cream together the butter, white sugar, and egg until light and fluffy.
4. In a separate bowl, whisk together the flour, nutmeg, cinnamon, baking soda, and baking powder.
5. Gradually add the dry ingredients to the creamed mixture, alternating with the reserved 1 cup of raisin water. Begin and end with the dry ingredients, mixing well after each addition.
6. Stir in the boiled raisins and chopped nuts.
7. Pour the batter into the prepared baking pan.
8. Bake in the preheated oven for 25-40 minutes or until a toothpick inserted into the center comes out clean. The baking time may vary depending on your oven, so check for doneness after 25 minutes and adjust accordingly.
9. Once done, remove the cake from the oven and allow it to cool in the pan for a few minutes before transferring it to a wire rack to cool completely.

## Fudge Icing

## Ingredients:

- 1/2 cup butter
- 1 cup brown sugar
- 1/4 cup milk
- 1 3/4 to 2 cups icing sugar

## Instructions:

1. In a saucepan, melt 1/2 cup of butter over low heat.
2. Stir in 1 cup of brown sugar and boil over low heat for 2 minutes, stirring constantly.
3. Add 1/4 cup of milk and bring the mixture to a boil again, continuing to stir constantly.
4. Gradually add 1 3/4 to 2 cups of icing sugar while beating until the icing is thick enough to spread.
5. If the icing becomes too stiff, you can add a little hot water to reach your desired consistency.
6. Once the cake has cooled completely, spread the fudge icing evenly over the top.
7. Slice and serve your delicious Raisin Cake with Fudge Icing.

Enjoy this delightful raisin cake with rich fudge icing as a sweet treat for any occasion!

**FOR DIABETICS:** not suggested.

# Cabbage Rolls

## Ingredients:

- 1 medium cabbage
- 1 lb ground hamburger
- 1 medium onion, chopped (about 1/2 cup)
- 1 tsp pepper
- 1 tsp salt
- 1 tsp mustard powder
- 1 cup cooked rice
- 1/2 cup brown sugar
- 1 tsp garlic
- 1 egg
- 1/4 cup fresh parsley, chopped (save some for garnish)

## Sauce for Cabbage Rolls:

- 2 tbsp butter
- 1/2 cup onion, chopped
- 1 tsp garlic
- 28 oz can of crushed tomatoes
- 15 oz can tomato sauce
- 2 tbsp brown sugar
- 1 tbsp red wine vinegar

## Instructions:

1. **Prepare the Cabbage:**
   - Core the medium cabbage and place it in the freezer. Allow it to freeze, then thaw it. This process will help soften the cabbage leaves, making them easier to work with.
2. **Prepare the Meat Mixture:**
   - In a mixing bowl, combine the ground hamburger, chopped onion, pepper, salt, mustard powder, cooked rice, brown sugar, garlic, egg, and 1/4 cup of chopped fresh parsley. Mix well until all the ingredients are evenly combined.

3. **Roll the Cabbage Rolls:**
   - Carefully peel off cabbage leaves one by one, making sure they are pliable.
   - Place a portion of the meat mixture onto each cabbage leaf.
   - Roll up the cabbage leaf around the meat, folding in the sides to enclose the filling, similar to rolling a burrito.

4. **Prepare the Sauce:**
   - In a saucepan, melt 2 tablespoons of butter, then sauté 1/2 cup of chopped onion and 1 teaspoon of garlic until the onion is translucent. Add crushed tomatoes, tomato sauce, brown sugar, and red wine vinegar. Simmer for 10-15 minutes.

5. **Assemble and Bake:**
   - Spread a bit of the prepared sauce on the bottom of a roasting pan.
   - Place the rolled cabbage rolls in the roasting pan.
   - Pour the sauce over the cabbage rolls, ensuring they are generously covered.
   - Cover the roasting pan with aluminum foil.

6. **Cooking:**
   - Preheat your oven to 350 degrees Fahrenheit (175 degrees Celsius).
   - Bake the cabbage rolls in the preheated oven for 1 1/2 to 2 hours. The cabbage rolls should be tender, and the meat filling should be thoroughly cooked.

7. **Serve:**
   - Sprinkle some fresh chopped parsley on top for garnish.

**FOR DIABETICS:** use an alternate sugar suggestion.

# Canning

Canning fruits is a
wonderful way to
preserve the flavors of
ripe and seasonal fruits
to enjoy throughout the
year. Below are basic
instructions for canning
fruits, along with some
specific recipes for
popular fruits like
peaches, strawberries,
and apples. Keep in
mind that canning
requires proper
equipment and safety
precautions, so be sure
to follow recommended
canning guidelines.

## Equipment:

- Canning jars with lids and bands
- Large stockpot or canner
- Cherry pitter (optional but recommended)
- Jar lifter
- Canning funnel
- Lid lifter
- Non-metallic utensil for removing air bubbles

## Basic Canning Instructions:

1. **Prepare Your Equipment:**
   - Wash and sterilize canning jars, lids, and bands in hot, soapy water. Rinse thoroughly.
2. **Prepare the Fruit:**
   - Wash, peel (if necessary), pit, and slice or dice the fruit as desired. Remove any bruised or damaged portions.

3. **Prepare Syrup (Optional):**
   - Some fruits are canned in syrup to preserve their quality. You can make a light, medium, or heavy syrup based on your preference. Bring the syrup ingredients (water and sugar) to a boil, stirring until the sugar dissolves. Reduce heat and keep it warm.

4. **Fill Jars:**
   - Pack the prepared fruit into hot, sterilized jars, leaving the recommended headspace (usually 1/2 to 1 inch) at the top. If using syrup, pour it over the fruit, leaving the same headspace.

5. **Remove Air Bubbles:**
   - Run a non-metallic utensil or a bubble remover tool along the inside of the jar to release any trapped air bubbles.

6. **Wipe Jar Rims:**
   - Use a clean, damp cloth to wipe the rims of the jars to ensure a clean seal.

7. **Apply Lids and Bands:**
   - Sterilize lids, and boil 5 minutes
   - Place sterilized lids on the jars and secure them with bands, tightening until they are "finger tight." Do not overtighten.

8. **Process Jars:**
   - Use a canner or large stockpot to process the jars. The processing time and method depend on the type of fruit and the jar size. Follow a tested canning recipe for specific instructions.

9. **Cool and Test Seals:**
   - After processing, remove the jars from the canner and allow them to cool on a clean towel or cooling rack. As they cool, you should hear the lids "ping," indicating a successful seal. Press down on the center of each lid to check for a firm, concave seal.

10. **Store Jars:**
    - Label the sealed jars with the contents and date. Store them in a cool, dark, and dry place.

Properly sealed jars can be stored for up to one year or more.

## Specific Canning Recipes:

### 1. Canned Peaches:

- Peel and pit ripe peaches.
- Prepare a light or medium syrup.
- Pack peaches into jars, leaving 1/2-inch headspace.
- Process in a boiling water bath for the recommended time based on jar size.

For Fruit Packed in Light Syrup (e.g., peaches, pears, apricots):

- Pint Jars: Process for approximately 20-25 minutes.
- Quart Jars: Process for approximately 25-30 minutes.

For Fruit Packed in Heavy Syrup (e.g., sweet cherries):

- Pint Jars: Process for approximately 20-25 minutes.
- Quart Jars: Process for approximately 25-30 minutes.

For Fruit Packed in Water (e.g., apples, berries):

- Pint Jars: Process for approximately 15-20 minutes.
- Quart Jars: Process for approximately 20-25 minutes.

### 2. Strawberry Jam:

- Hull and chop strawberries.
- Mix strawberries and sugar in a large pot.
- Cook until thickened.

- Ladle hot jam into jars and process in a boiling water bath.

Pint Jars:

- Process for approximately 5-10 minutes.

Half-Pint Jars:

- Process for approximately 5-10 minutes.

## 3. Canned Applesauce:

- Peel, core, and slice apples.
- Cook apples with water until soft.
- Mash or blend cooked apples into sauce.
- Ladle hot applesauce into jars and process in a boiling water bath.

For Plain Applesauce:

- Pint Jars: Process for approximately 15-20 minutes.
- Quart Jars: Process for approximately 20-25 minutes.

## 4. Canned Cherries:

- Fresh cherries
- Water
- Sugar (optional)
- Syrup for 7 jars – Boil 12 cups water & 4 cups sugar

For Sweet Cherries (Packed in Syrup):

- Pint Jars: Process for approximately 20-25 minutes.
- Quart Jars: Process for approximately 25-30 minutes.

For Sour Cherries (Packed in Syrup):

- Pint Jars: Process for approximately 20-25 minutes.
- Quart Jars: Process for approximately 25-30 minutes.

Here's a simple SYRUP RECIPE that you can use for canning peaches, cherries, pears, and other fruits. This syrup provides a light sweetness to the fruits without overpowering their natural flavor. You can adjust the sweetness to your preference by varying the sugar-to-water ratio.

## Ingredients:

- 5 cups water
- 2 1/4 cups granulated sugar

## Instructions:

1. In a large saucepan, combine the water and sugar. Stir well to dissolve the sugar.
2. Place the saucepan over medium-high heat and bring the mixture to a boil. Stir occasionally to ensure that the sugar is completely dissolved.
3. Once the syrup comes to a boil, reduce the heat to low and let it simmer for about 5 minutes, stirring occasionally. This brief simmer helps ensure the sugar is fully dissolved and the syrup is well-blended.
4. Remove the syrup from the heat and allow it to cool slightly. You can use it warm or let it cool to room temperature before using it for canning.
5. To can fruits with this syrup, pack the prepared fruits into hot, sterilized jars, leaving the recommended headspace. Pour the warm syrup over the fruits, ensuring that they are fully covered while leaving about 1/2 inch of headspace.
6. Follow the specific canning instructions for the type of fruit you're canning, including processing times and methods.
7. Wipe the jar rims, place sterilized lids and bands on the jars, and process them according to the recommended canning guidelines.

This syrup can be used for canning peaches, cherries, pears, and many other fruits. Adjust the sweetness by using more or less sugar according to your taste preferences. Always follow proper canning procedures and guidelines to ensure the safety and preservation of your canned fruits.

**FOR DIABETICS: not suggested.**

# Better Than "Sex" Chocolate Cake

## Ingredients:

For the Cake:

- Bake cake or use 1 box of chocolate cake mix (plus ingredients needed for the mix, typically eggs, water, and oil)
- 1 can sweetened condensed milk (14 ounces)
- 1 jar caramel topping (12 ounces)
- 1 container whipped topping (e.g., Cool Whip) (8 ounces)
- 1 cup toffee bits or crushed Heath bars

## Instructions:

Bake the Cake:

1. Preheat your oven to the temperature specified on the cake mix box.
2. Prepare a 9x13-inch baking pan by greasing it or lining it with parchment paper.
3. Follow the instructions on the cake mix box to prepare the chocolate cake batter.
4. Pour the cake batter into the prepared baking pan and bake it according to the package instructions.
5. Once the cake is baked and a toothpick inserted into the center comes out clean, remove it from the oven and let it cool for a few minutes.

Poke Holes:

6. While the cake is still warm, use the end of a wooden spoon or a fork to poke holes all over the cake.

Add Sweetened Condensed Milk and Caramel:

7. Pour the entire can of sweetened condensed milk evenly over the cake, making sure it fills the holes.
8. Next, drizzle the caramel topping over the cake, also ensuring it gets into the holes.

Cool:

9. Allow the cake to cool completely in the pan. This may take a couple of hours.

Top with Whipped Topping and Toffee:

10. Once the cake has cooled, spread the whipped topping evenly over the cake.
11. Sprinkle the toffee bits or crushed Heath bars over the whipped topping, creating a delicious and crunchy topping.

Chill:

12. For the best results, refrigerate the cake for several hours or overnight to allow the flavors to meld and the cake to set.

Serve:

13. Slice and serve your "Better Than Sex" Chocolate Cake to your delighted guests.

**FOR DIABETICS:** not suggested.

How does a cucumber become a pickle?

It goes through a jarring experience!

# My Daughter's Recipes

## Alicia

In the tapestry of our family, my daughter stands as a radiant thread woven with the gifts of eloquence and a profound understanding of nourishing one's body and soul. Even from a tender age, she exhibited a remarkable awareness of what 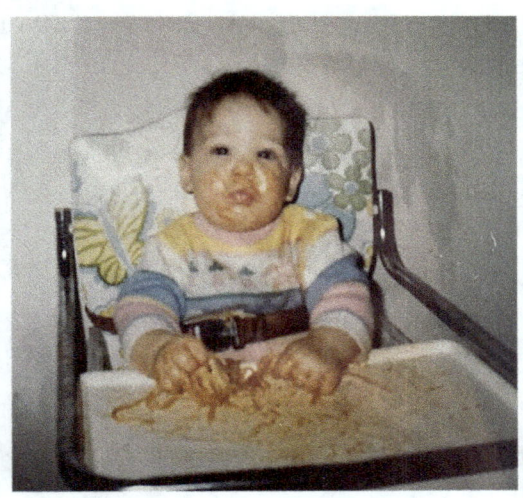 she consumed, revealing a unique connection to the concept of healthy eating. As I reflect on the journey we've shared, I am filled with gratitude for the precious moments we've experienced together.

From the earliest years, my daughter's consciousness about the foods she consumed was a beacon of inspiration. Her choices were a testament to her innate wisdom, a testament to the way she intuited the impact of what she put into her body. These early expressions of her care and consideration for her well-being were a testament to her character and the path she would eventually embrace.

As she grew and flourished, our time together deepened our bond. Now, as she nurtures her own growing family, her commitment to wholesome living and nourishing meals remains steadfast. Her home is a haven of mindful nourishment, and every meal prepared carries the intention of nourishing not only bodies but also spirits.

One of the many treasures she shares with us is her salads, vibrant compositions that elevate every meal they accompany. These salads are a reflection of her culinary artistry, a palette of colors and textures that tantalize the senses and delight the palate. With every bite, we taste her dedication to creating meals that are both healthful and delicious.

As a grandmother, watching my daughter nourish her own children with the same care and love she extended for her own well-being is a source of immense joy. It's a testament to the legacy of mindful eating that she continues to weave, passing down not only the wisdom of nourishing foods but also the significance of caring for oneself and one's loved ones.

Through her journey, my daughter has embraced a path that seamlessly integrates the art of words and the science of nourishment. Her commitment to healthy eating and nurturing relationships resonates deeply, reminding us that the act of nourishing goes beyond the physical and extends to the emotional and spiritual realms as well.

I am filled with pride as I witness her journey as a mother, a nurturer, and a guardian of well-being. Her salads are more than just dishes; they symbolize a philosophy of care and an unwavering dedication to the wellness of her family and those she loves. As I savor each salad she crafts, I taste the essence of her journey—the wisdom, the love, and the legacy that continues to unfold in every colorful leaf and every vibrant bite.

My Grand Babies

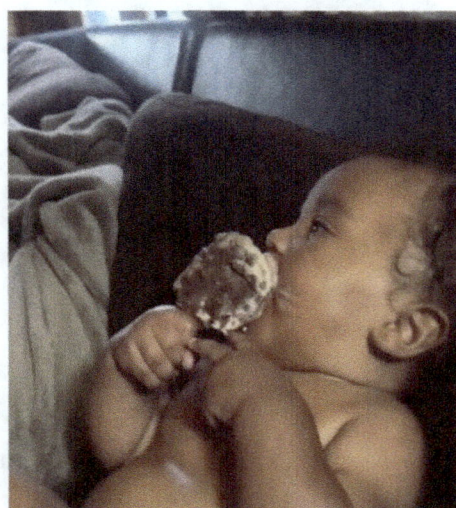

DeMelo devoured his first ice cream, daddy said he cried for more. He loves any type of food, *okay maybe not hidden veggies like squash in his fruit puree.*

His big brother, DeJounté on the other hand is a picky eater. But he loves his beef *(joke is Alicia hates beef. I used to have to cook her a piece of chicken when we ate red meat – Karma's a b\*tch).*

# Stir Fry

## Ingredients:

- 1 pound pork, chicken, and yes, even beef
- 1 tablespoon vegetable oil (for cooking)
- 2 cloves garlic, minced
- 1 teaspoon ginger, minced (optional)
- 1/4 cup soy sauce (or to taste)
- 1 medium head of cauliflower, riced (about 4 cups)
- 2 cups mixed vegetables (such as bell peppers, broccoli, carrots, snap peas, or any of your favorites)
- Salt and pepper to taste
- Green onions or cilantro for garnish (optional)

## Instructions:

1. **Prepare the Cauliflower Rice:** Cut the cauliflower into florets and place them in a food processor. Pulse until it reaches a rice-like consistency. You can also use a box grater to rice the cauliflower manually.
2. **Stir-Fry the Ground Meat:** In a large skillet or wok, heat the vegetable oil over medium-high heat. Add the ground pork or chicken, breaking it apart as it cooks. Cook until browned and cooked through, about 5-7 minutes. If you're using chicken, make sure it's no longer pink in the center.
3. **Add Garlic and Ginger:** Stir in the minced garlic and ginger (if using) and cook for an additional 30 seconds until fragrant.
4. **Soy Sauce:** Pour the soy sauce over the cooked meat and stir to combine. Adjust the amount of soy sauce to your taste.
5. **Add Vegetables:** Add your choice of mixed vegetables to the skillet or wok. Stir-fry for about 3-4 minutes or until the vegetables are tender-crisp. You can use fresh or frozen vegetables, depending on your preference.
6. **Cauliflower Rice:** Add the riced cauliflower to the skillet. Stir-fry for another 3-4 minutes or until the cauliflower rice is heated through and has a slightly tender texture—season with salt and pepper to taste.

7. **Garnish and Serve:** If desired, garnish your stir-fry with chopped green onions or fresh cilantro. Serve hot and enjoy!

This stir-fry is versatile, and you can customize it with your favorite vegetables and seasonings. It's a low-carb and flavorful option for a quick and healthy meal.

**FOR DIABETICS:** enjoy!

One of Alicia's favs', Beef and Broccoli

# Week Dinner Prep

Meal prepping for the week can help you maintain a healthy and convenient eating routine. Here are some suggestions for meal prepping healthy dinners for the week:

**Proteins** (Meat or Plant-Based):

1. Grilled Chicken: Marinate chicken breasts or thighs with your favorite seasonings, then grill or bake them. Slice into portions for each day.
2. Baked Salmon: Season salmon fillets with herbs and spices, then bake until flaky. Salmon is a great source of omega-3 fatty acids.
3. Tofu Stir-Fry: Cube tofu and stir-fry with mixed vegetables in a healthy stir-fry sauce for a plant-based protein option.
4. Lean Ground Turkey: Cook ground turkey with spices and use it as a base for various dishes like turkey tacos, chili, or turkey meatballs.

**Vegetables:**

1. Roasted Vegetables: Roast a variety of colorful vegetables like carrots, broccoli, and bell peppers with olive oil and seasonings.
2. Steamed Vegetables: Steam green beans, cauliflower, or Brussels sprouts and season them lightly with salt and pepper.
3. Sauteed Spinach: Quickly sauté fresh spinach with garlic for a nutritious side.
4. Mixed Salad: Prepare a mixed green salad with ingredients like spinach, lettuce, cherry tomatoes, cucumber, and bell peppers. Store the salad dressing separately to keep it fresh.

**Carbohydrates (Optional):**

1. Quinoa: Cook a batch of quinoa to use as a side dish or a base for various meals.
2. Sweet Potatoes: Bake or roast sweet potatoes for a healthy source of complex carbohydrates.
3. Brown Rice: Cook brown rice to add to your meals for extra fiber.

**Meal Ideas:**

1. Grilled Chicken with Roasted Vegetables: Pair grilled chicken with a side of roasted vegetables. Drizzle with olive oil and add your favorite herbs.
2. Salmon with Quinoa and Steamed Broccoli: Serve baked salmon with a side of quinoa and steamed broccoli.
3. Tofu Stir-Fry with Brown Rice: Combine tofu stir-fry with brown rice for a plant-based meal.
4. Turkey Taco Bowls: Use the ground turkey to create taco bowls with brown rice, black beans, lettuce, and salsa.

**Extras:**

1. Hummus: Include hummus and whole-grain crackers or sliced veggies as a healthy snack option.
2. Greek Yogurt: Have Greek yogurt and fresh berries for a quick and nutritious dessert.

Note: store your prepped meals in airtight containers and refrigerate them promptly. You can mix and match the proteins, vegetables, and carbohydrates throughout the week to create different meal combinations, keeping your dinners interesting and healthy.

**FOR DIABETICS: enjoy!**

# Salad Prep

Salad prep is a great way to ensure you have fresh and healthy salads ready to enjoy throughout the week. Here's how you can prepare salads for the week:

## Ingredients:

1. Leafy Greens: Choose a variety of greens, such as lettuce, spinach, kale, or arugula, as the base of your salads.
2. Vegetables: Select a mix of colorful vegetables like bell peppers, cucumbers, tomatoes, carrots, broccoli, and radishes. Chop or slice them as needed.
3. Protein: Add a source of protein to your salads. Options include grilled chicken, roasted chickpeas, hard-boiled eggs, tofu, or canned tuna or salmon.
4. Nuts and Seeds: Consider adding some crunch and healthy fats with ingredients like almonds, walnuts, sunflower seeds, or pumpkin seeds.
5. Fruits: Add sweetness and extra nutrients with fresh fruits like strawberries, blueberries, apples or oranges.
6. Cheese (Optional): If you enjoy cheese, add a sprinkle of feta, goat cheese, or grated Parmesan.
7. Dressing: Prepare a homemade salad dressing or have store-bought options on hand. Popular choices include balsamic vinaigrette, ranch or olive oil, and vinegar.

## Salad Assembly:

1. Start with a clean and dry container with an airtight lid. Mason jars or meal prep containers work well for this purpose.
2. Begin by adding the salad dressing to the bottom of the container. This prevents the greens from getting soggy prematurely.
3. Layer your ingredients strategically. Start with the heartier and moisture-resistant ingredients at the bottom. For example, add proteins like chicken or beans first, followed by vegetables, fruits, nuts, seeds, and finally, the leafy greens on top.

4. Seal the container tightly and store it in the refrigerator.

**Tips:**

1. Keep ingredients separate: If you want to maintain the crispness of certain ingredients, such as lettuce or nuts, consider keeping them separate from the dressing until you're ready to eat. You can use small containers or plastic bags for this purpose.
2. Portion control: Use containers that provide portion control. This helps ensure you have the right serving size for each salad.
3. Customize as needed: While prepping, customize each salad to your liking. You can vary the ingredients and dressings to keep your meals interesting.
4. Eat within the week: Consume your prepped salads within the week to ensure they stay fresh and safe to eat.
5. Refresh as needed: If your salad includes ingredients that may wilt, like lettuce, you can refresh them by adding an ice pack to your lunch bag.

By prepping salads in advance, you'll have a convenient and nutritious option ready for your meals, making it easier to stick to your healthy eating goals.

**FOR DIABETICS: enjoy!**

What's a salad's favorite song?

"Lettuce Entertain You"!

# My Son and Daughter-In-Law's Recipes

## Colten - Pizza

He said his favorite recipe is: Buy a frozen pizza and put it in the oven at 400°F (200°C) for 12 minutes. Done!

Making pizza at home can be a fun and delicious experience. While it's perfectly fine to enjoy a frozen pizza, see Aunt Iris's basic homemade pizza recipe that you can try if you ever want to make one from scratch:

**FOR DIABETICS**: substitute for a cauliflower pizza shell or "ritzza pizza."

## FROM COLTEN'S CLASSMATE'S MOMS

# Seafood Linguine (Jesse)

## Ingredients:

- 1/4 cup chopped onion
- 1/2 cup green pepper
- 2 tablespoons butter
- 1/2 cup milk
- 8 ounces cream cheese
- 1 tablespoon garlic salt
- 2 cups assorted seafood (shrimp, scallops, crab, etc.)
- 1 can whole mushrooms
- 2 tablespoons parsley
- 375g linguine pasta
- 1/4 cup grated Parmesan cheese
- 1 teaspoon dried dill

## Instructions:

1. Cook the linguine pasta according to the package instructions until al dente. Drain and set aside.

2. In a large skillet, melt the butter over medium heat. Add the chopped onion and green pepper. Sauté until they become tender, usually for about 5 minutes.
3. Reduce the heat to low. Add the milk, cream cheese, and garlic salt to the skillet. Stir constantly until the cream cheese is melted and the mixture becomes creamy and smooth.
4. Stir in the assorted seafood and canned mushrooms. Cook for an additional 5-7 minutes or until the seafood is heated through and cooked.
5. Add the cooked linguine pasta to the skillet, tossing to combine with the seafood mixture. Cook for an additional 2-3 minutes to heat the pasta.
6. Sprinkle in the dried dill and parsley. Stir well to combine.
7. Serve the seafood linguine hot, garnished with grated Parmesan cheese on top.

# Fettuccine With Seafood (Sharay)

## Ingredients:

- 1/4 cup (60g) butter
- 1 cup (250ml) whipping cream
- 1 cup (250ml) milk
- 1 cup (250ml) grated Parmesan cheese
- 1/2 teaspoon (2.5ml) nutmeg
- Salt and pepper to taste
- Assorted seafood (shrimp, scallops, crab, etc.)
- 8 ounces (225g) fettuccine pasta, cooked and drained

## Instructions:

1. In a large skillet or saucepan, melt the butter over medium heat.
2. Add the whipping cream and milk to the melted butter. Stir continuously and bring the mixture to a gentle simmer. Allow it to simmer for a few minutes until it thickens slightly.

3. Stir in the grated Parmesan cheese and continue to cook, stirring frequently, until the cheese has completely melted and the sauce is smooth and creamy.
4. Season the sauce with nutmeg, salt, and pepper to taste. Adjust the seasonings according to your preference.
5. Add your choice of assorted seafood to the sauce. Continue to cook for a few minutes until the seafood is heated through and cooked. Be careful not to overcook the seafood.
6. While preparing the sauce and seafood, cook the fettuccine pasta according to the package instructions until it's al dente. Drain the pasta.
7. Combine the cooked and drained fettuccine with the seafood and creamy sauce. Toss gently to coat the pasta evenly with the sauce.
8. Serve your Fettuccine with Seafood hot, garnished with additional Parmesan cheese and freshly chopped parsley if desired.

**FOR DIABETICS**: Both are not suggested.

# Morgan's Warm Artichoke Dip

Morgan's Recipes (my daughter-n-law)

(Yields 2 ½ cups)

## Ingredients:

- 1 package (8 oz) of softened Philadelphia cream cheese
- 1 can (14 oz) of chopped and drained artichoke hearts
- ½ cup of Kraft Mayo
- ½ cup of Kraft 100% grated parmesan cheese
- 1 minced clove of garlic

## Instructions:

1. Combine all the ingredients using an electric mixer on medium speed until thoroughly blended.
2. Spoon the mixture into a 9-inch pie plate or quiche dish.
3. Bake in a preheated oven at 350 degrees F for 20-25 minutes or until it's lightly browned on the surface.
4. Serve the dip with vegetable dippers or homemade baked pita wedges.

## To Make Baked Pita Wedges:

1. Cut 3 split pita breads into 8 triangles each.
2. Place the pita triangles on a cookie sheet and bake at 350 degrees F for 10-12 minutes or until they become crisp.

**FOR DIABETICS**: see nut crackers.

# Mexican-Style Lasagna

## Ingredients:

- 1.5 lbs ground turkey
- 1 cup each of diced red onions and diced green bell pepper
- 2 teaspoons minced garlic
- 1 cup canned black beans, rinsed and drained
- 1 cup diced tomatoes
- ½ cup frozen or canned corn
- 1 ½ teaspoons chili powder
- 1 teaspoon ground cumin
- 2 cups of your preferred tomato pasta sauce
- 1 cup medium salsa
- ¼ teaspoon ground black pepper
- 2 tablespoons minced fresh cilantro
- 4 large or 8 small whole wheat tortillas
- 1 ½ cups tightly packed shredded aged cheddar cheese
- ¼ cup chopped green onions
- 1 cup sour cream (optional)

Filling: The filling on its own makes an exceptional chili!

## Instructions:

To make the Filling:

1. In a large, non-stick pot or skillet, cook the ground turkey, red onions, green bell pepper, and garlic over medium-high heat until the turkey is no longer pink. While cooking, break up any large pieces of turkey.
2. Add the black beans, diced tomatoes, corn, chili powder, and ground cumin. Cook and stir for an additional 2 minutes.
3. Incorporate the pasta sauce, salsa, and black pepper. Bring the mixture to a boil, then reduce the heat to low. Cover and simmer for 5 minutes, stirring occasionally. Stir in the minced cilantro and remove it from the heat.


To Assemble the Casserole:

4. Preheat your oven to 375 degrees F. Grease a 9 x 13-inch casserole dish with cooking spray.
5. Spread one-third of the sauce mixture over the bottom of the casserole dish.
6. Arrange half of the tortillas on top, overlapping and trimming as needed to fit.
7. Layer on one-third of the sauce mixture, followed by half of the shredded cheese.
8. Place the remaining tortillas on top, and then layer on the remaining sauce.
9. Sprinkle the remaining cheese over the sauce and garnish with chopped green onions.
10. Cover the casserole with foil and bake for 35 minutes. Uncover and bake for an additional 10 minutes.
11. Allow the Mexican-style layered casserole to rest for at least 10 minutes before slicing, making it easier to serve.
12. Optionally, top each portion with a dollop of sour cream.


**FOR DIABETICS**: enjoy!

What's a pie's favorite line in a movie?

"Cut! Cut! Cut!"

# My Sister's Recipes

## Kandus's Broccoli Casserole

**Ingredients:**

- 2 heads of fresh broccoli, cut into florets
- 1 onion, chopped
- 2 cloves garlic, minced
- 2 tablespoons butter
- 1 can of cream of mushroom soup
- 1 small can of Cheese Whiz or cheese sauce
- Crumbled crackers (for topping)
- Sliced almonds (for topping)

## Instructions:

1.  Preheat your oven to 350°F (175°C).
2.  Steam or blanch the broccoli florets until they are slightly tender. Drain them and set them aside.
3.  In a skillet or frying pan, melt the 2 tablespoons of butter over medium heat.
4.  Add the chopped onion and minced garlic to the melted butter. Sauté them until they become translucent and fragrant, typically for about 2-3 minutes.
5.  Stir in the can of cream of mushroom soup and the small can of Cheese Whiz (or cheese sauce) into the onion and garlic mixture. Continue to cook and stir until the ingredients are well combined and heated through. This will create a creamy cheese sauce.
6.  In a greased 9x13-inch baking dish, arrange the steamed broccoli florets evenly.
7.  Pour the creamy cheese sauce mixture over the broccoli, making sure all the florets are well coated.
8.  Bake the casserole in the preheated oven for approximately 30 minutes.
9.  In the last 15 minutes of baking, top the casserole with a layer of crumbled crackers and sliced almonds. This will add a crunchy and flavorful topping to the dish.
10. Continue baking for the remaining 15 minutes or until the top is golden brown and the casserole is bubbling.
11. Remove the broccoli casserole from the oven and let it cool for a few minutes before serving.
12. Serve your delicious and cheesy Broccoli Casserole as a side dish or a comforting main course.

Enjoy this creamy and flavorful broccoli casserole, which is perfect for gatherings, holiday dinners, or any occasion when you want a comforting and satisfying dish.

**FOR DIABETICS:** If you're looking to replace crumbled crackers in a recipe for a diabetic-friendly broccoli casserole, consider using alternatives that are lower in carbohydrates and have a lower impact on blood sugar levels. Here are some options:

- **Almond Flour or Almond Meal:** Almond flour or almond meal can be used as a low-carb replacement for crumbled crackers. They provide a nutty flavor and a nice crunch. Simply sprinkle almond flour or meal over the casserole before baking.
- **Ground Flaxseed:** Ground flaxseed is high in fiber and healthy fats, making it a nutritious option. It can add a subtle nutty flavor and a pleasant texture to the casserole. Use it as a topping.
- **Chopped Nuts:** Chopped nuts, such as almonds, pecans, or walnuts, can be an excellent alternative to crumbled crackers. They offer a satisfying crunch and healthy fats. Spread a layer of chopped nuts over the casserole before baking.
- **Parmesan Cheese:** Grated Parmesan cheese can create a crispy and savory topping. It's low in carbs and adds a rich flavor. Sprinkle grated Parmesan over the casserole during the last 15 minutes of baking.
- **Pork Rinds:** Crushed pork rinds can mimic the texture of traditional breadcrumbs or crackers while being very low in carbs. They are a popular choice for low-carb and keto-friendly recipes.
- **Ground Pork Rinds:** Similar to crushed pork rinds, ground pork rinds can be used as a coating for a crispy topping. They work well in savory dishes.
- **Coconut Flakes**: Unsweetened coconut flakes can add a unique texture and a subtle sweetness to your casserole. Use them sparingly, as coconut does contain natural sugars.

# Tracy's Shrimp Fundido

For those that remember Jonathan L. Segals restaurant, she said this recipe was gifted to her in the early 1990s.

## Ingredients:

- 2 tablespoons butter
- 1 teaspoon flour

For the Vegetables:

- 1/4 cup diced onions
- 1/4 cup diced tomatoes
- 1/4 cup crushed garlic
- A couple of handfuls of fresh spinach

For the Seasonings:

- ½ tsp Chili powder
- ½ tsp Garlic powder
- ½ tsp Mustard powder

For the Shrimp and Cheese:

- 2 cans of small shrimp
- A few peeled large shrimp
- 1 cup grated Havarti or Gouda cheese (or a combination)
- Sharp or old cheddar cheese (or a combination)

## Instructions:

1. Preheat your oven to 350°F (175°C).
2. In a saucepan that can go into the oven, melt 2 tablespoons of butter over very low heat, stirring.
3. Add 1 teaspoon of flour to the melted butter and continue stirring. Cook the flour for a minute or so until it's well combined and slightly thickened.
4. Add diced onions, diced tomatoes, and crushed garlic to the saucepan. Cook all the ingredients slowly over very low heat, stirring occasionally.
5. Once the vegetables have softened, add a couple of handfuls of fresh spinach to the mixture. Cover and continue cooking for another 10 minutes, stirring occasionally, until the spinach is wilted.
6. Season the mixture with chili powder, garlic powder, and mustard powder to taste. Adjust the seasonings to your preference.
7. Stir in the small shrimp and add the peeled large shrimp to the mixture.
8. Sprinkle the grated Havarti or Gouda cheese (or a combination) over the top of the mixture.
9. Heavily sprinkle sharp or old cheddar cheese (or a combination) on top of everything.
10. Transfer the saucepan to the preheated oven and bake for 10 minutes or until the cheese is melted and bubbly and the shrimp are cooked through.
11. Carefully remove the saucepan from the oven and serve the Shrimp Fundido hot, either on its own or with your choice of accompaniments like tortilla chips, crusty bread, or rice.

**FOR DIABETICS:** enjoy!

Why did the friends invite their
favorite dishes to the family
barbecue?
Because they wanted
to have a
"taste-imonial" reunion!

# Friends and Other Family Member's Recipes

## Roselie's Mom's (Lorraine) Antipasto

Alicia's Godmother

**Ingredients:**

- 1 lb cauliflower, chopped into small bite-size pieces
- 1 small jar of tiny white onions
- 1 32 oz jar of dill pickles
- 1 tin of black pitted olives
- 1 tin of pitted green olives
- 1 green pepper, diced
- 1 red pepper, diced
- 1 can of mushrooms
- 4 tins of anchovies
- 2 tins of tuna
- 1 can of crabmeat
- 30 oz (3 3/4 cups) of ketchup
- ½ cup olive oil
- ½ cup white vinegar

## Instructions:

1. Begin by preparing your ingredients. Chop the cauliflower into small bite-size pieces, drain and rinse the tiny white onions, and drain the dill pickles, black olives, green olives, mushrooms, anchovies, tuna, and crabmeat. Dice the green and red peppers, setting aside all the components for the recipe.
2. In a large pot over medium heat, combine the chopped cauliflower, tiny white onions, diced green and red peppers, black olives, green olives, mushrooms, anchovies, tuna, and crabmeat.
3. In a separate bowl, mix together the ketchup, olive oil, and white vinegar until well combined. This tangy tomato sauce will infuse your medley with delightful flavors.
4. Pour the ketchup mixture over the ingredients in the pot. Stir gently to ensure the sauce coats all the elements evenly.
5. Bring the mixture to a gentle boil, stirring constantly to prevent sticking or burning. The aromatic blend of ingredients will begin to meld together, creating a symphony of savory aromas.
6. Continue to simmer the mixture, stirring occasionally, for about 15-20 minutes. The flavors will blend beautifully, and the cauliflower will become tender yet retain a satisfying bite.
7. As the mixture cooks, prepare your pint jars by sterilizing them according to standard canning procedures.
8. Once the cauliflower medley is cooked to perfection, carefully ladle it into the prepared pint jars, leaving about ½-inch of headspace at the top.
9. Seal the jars with sterilized lids and rings, ensuring they are closed tightly.
10. Process the sealed pint jars in a boiling water bath for 30 minutes, following recommended canning guidelines.
11. After processing, carefully remove the jars from the water bath and allow them to cool on a clean towel or cooling rack.
12. As the jars cool, you may hear the satisfying "pop" of the lids sealing—a sure sign that your culinary creation is ready for future enjoyment.

**FOR DIABETICS:** enjoy!

# Roselie's Baked Oatmeal

## Ingredients:

- 1 cup oil (or 1/2 cup oil + 1/2 cup unsweetened applesauce for a lighter option)
- 1 cup sugar or alternative
- 4 eggs
- 1 teaspoon salt
- 1 teaspoon ground cinnamon
- 4 teaspoons baking powder
- 2 cups milk
- 2 chopped apples
- 1 cup cranberries
- 1 cup combined fresh or frozen blueberries, peaches, rhubarb, or any other fruit you prefer
- 6 cups rolled oats
- Optional: 1 cup ground flaxseed, sliced almonds, or protein powder for added nutrition

## Instructions:

1. Preheat your oven to 400°F (200°C). Grease a 9x13-inch baking pan.
2. In a large mixing bowl, beat together the oil (or oil and applesauce combination) and sugar until well combined.
3. Add the eggs, one at a time, mixing well after each addition.
4. Stir in the salt, ground cinnamon, and baking powder until evenly incorporated.
5. Pour in the milk and mix until you have a smooth batter.
6. If you're adding optional ingredients like ground flaxseed, sliced almonds, or protein powder for added nutrition, fold them into the batter at this point.
7. Gently fold in the chopped apples, cranberries, and your chosen combination of additional fruits.
8. Finally, add the rolled oats to the mixture, making sure everything is well combined.
9. Pour the prepared mixture into the greased 9x13-inch baking pan, spreading it out evenly.

10. Bake in the preheated oven for approximately 35-45 minutes or until the top is golden brown and the oatmeal is set in the center. The exact baking time may vary, so keep an eye on it.
11. Once done, remove the baked oatmeal from the oven and allow it to cool slightly before serving.
12. Serve warm, and if desired, you can top individual servings with a drizzle of maple syrup, a dollop of Greek yogurt, or a sprinkle of fresh berries.

Roselie's Baked Oatmeal is a comforting and wholesome breakfast option that's perfect for a cozy morning with family or friends. It's packed with flavor and nutrition from the oats and a variety of fruits. Enjoy!

**FOR DIABETICS:** enjoy!

# Roselie's Mom's Bran Muffins

## Ingredients:

- 2 cups All-Bran cereal
- 2 cups boiling water
- 1 cup (2 sticks) butter
- 3 cups sugar
- 4 cups buttermilk
- 5 cups all-purpose flour
- 3 tablespoons baking soda
- 1 tablespoon salt
- 4 cups bran flake cereal
- 2 cups raisins and/or cranberries

## Instructions:

1. Preheat and Prep: Preheat your oven to 400°F (200°C). Line muffin tins with paper liners or grease them if you prefer.
2. Soak All-Bran: In a large mixing bowl, place 2 cups of All-Bran cereal. Pour the boiling water over it and stir. Let it sit to soak and soften while you prepare the other ingredients.
3. Cream Butter and Sugar: In another large mixing bowl, cream together the butter and sugar until it's light and fluffy.
4. Add Buttermilk: Blend in the buttermilk with the creamed butter and sugar mixture.
5. Combine Dry Ingredients: In a separate bowl, sift together the flour, baking soda, and salt.
6. Mix Wet and Dry Ingredients: Gradually add the dry ingredients to the butter-sugar-buttermilk mixture. Stir until just combined.
7. Add Soaked All-Bran: Stir in the soaked All-Bran cereal.
8. Fold in Cereal and Fruit: Gently fold in the bran flake cereal and the raisins/cranberries.

9.  Fill Muffin Tins: Fill the prepared muffin tins about two-thirds full with the muffin batter.
10. Bake: Bake in the preheated oven for 15-20 minutes or until a toothpick inserted into the center of a muffin comes out clean.
11. Cool: Allow the muffins to cool in the tins for a few minutes before transferring them to a wire rack to cool completely.
12. Store: These muffins are known for getting even better after a day, so cover them and keep them in the refrigerator for 24 hours. They can also be stored in an airtight container in the fridge for up to eight weeks.

Makes 50+ muffins.

**FOR DIABETICS:** not suggested!

# Roselie's Best Pie Crust

## Ingredients:

- 3 ¾ cups all-purpose flour
- 1 tablespoon sugar
- ½ to 1 tablespoon salt (adjust to taste)
- ½ teaspoon baking powder
- 1 ¾ cups cold unsalted butter, cubed
- 2/3 cup ice-cold water
- 2 tablespoons sour cream or plain yogurt
- 1 teaspoon vinegar (white or apple cider)

## Instructions:

1. **Prepare the Dry Ingredients:** In a large mixing bowl, combine the flour, sugar, salt, and baking powder. Stir them together until well-mixed.
2. **Cut in the Butter:** Add the cold, cubed butter to the dry ingredients. Use a pastry blender or two forks to cut the butter into the flour mixture. Continue until the mixture resembles coarse crumbs with pea-sized or smaller butter chunks.
3. **Mix the Wet Ingredients:** In a separate small bowl, combine the ice-cold water, sour cream (or yogurt), and vinegar.
4. **Add the Liquid:** Pour the liquid mixture all at once into the flour-butter mixture. Quickly stir with a fork until the dough starts to come together. Do not overmix; it's okay if it's a bit crumbly.
5. **Form the Dough:** Gather the dough into a ball. If needed, you can lightly knead it a few times to bring it together. Divide the dough in half to make two crusts.
6. **Chill the Dough:** Wrap each half of the dough separately in plastic wrap or cellophane. Refrigerate for at least 2 hours or overnight. If you freeze it, thaw it overnight in the refrigerator.
7. **Roll the Dough:** Roll out one portion of the chilled dough on a floured surface to your desired thickness (usually about ¼ inch). Be sure to turn the dough as you roll to prevent sticking.

8. **Transfer to Pie Plate:** Carefully transfer the rolled dough to a pie plate. Do not stretch it when placing it on the plate.
9. **Add Filling:** Add your desired pie filling. If it's a fruit pie, you can add up to 2 cups more fruit as it cooks down during baking.
10. **Top Crust** (if making a double-crust pie): If you're making a double-crust pie, roll out the second portion of dough and place it on top of the filling. Mold the top crust to the edges of the bottom crust, creating hills and valleys.
11. **Optional Glaze:** For a shiny top crust, beat 1 egg with 1 tablespoon of whipping cream and brush it on top of the crust before baking. You can also sprinkle sugar and cinnamon on top if desired.
12. **Bake:** Follow your specific pie recipe for baking instructions, as baking times and temperatures can vary based on the filling.

This classic pie crust recipe should yield a flaky, delicious crust for your homemade pies.

**FOR DIABETICS:** not suggested.

# Roselie's Apple Pie

## Ingredients:

- 5-6 cups of peeled and sliced apples (use a mixture of varieties like Granny Smith, Fuji, or Honeycrisp)
- 1 cup brown sugar
- 1 tablespoon lemon or orange juice
- 2-3 teaspoons ground cinnamon (adjust to taste)
- 1/4 teaspoon ground nutmeg
- 1/4 cup all-purpose flour
- 2 tablespoons cornstarch
- 1/4 cup butter, cubed
- 1 or 2 pie crusts (for a double-crust or lattice pie)

## Instructions:

1.  Preheat the Oven: Preheat your oven to 400°F (200°C).
2.  Prepare the Pie Crust: If you're making a double-crust pie, prepare your pie crusts. Roll out one of the crusts and place it in a 9-inch pie plate. Trim any excess hanging over the edge. If you like, you can use the second crust for a lattice top or a full top crust.
3.  Prepare the Apples: Peel, core, and slice the apples into chunks. You can adjust the thickness of the slices to your preference.
4.  Mix the Filling: In a large bowl, combine the sliced apples, brown sugar, lemon or orange juice, ground cinnamon, ground nutmeg, all-purpose flour, and cornstarch. Toss everything together until the apples are well coated.
5.  Fill the Pie: Pour the apple mixture into the prepared pie crust. If you're using a top crust, add it now. If you're making a lattice top, create a lattice pattern with strips of pie crust.
6.  Dot with Butter: Distribute the cubed butter evenly over the top of the apple filling.
7.  Seal and Vent: If using a double-crust, seal the edges by pressing them together and then crimp the edges decoratively. If using a full top crust, make a few slits or cutouts in the top crust to allow steam to escape.
8.  Bake: Place the pie in the preheated oven. Bake at 400°F (200°C) for 15 minutes to set the crust, then reduce the oven temperature to 350°F (175°C). Continue baking for another 50 minutes or until the filling is bubbly and the crust is golden brown.
9.  Cool and Serve: Allow the pie to cool for a while before serving. This pie is delicious on its own or with a scoop of vanilla ice cream.

**FOR DIABETICS:** not suggested.

# Lydia's Shortbread

She was like family. She worked for me from 1999-2012

## Ingredients:

- 1 pound (4 sticks) soft butter
- ½ cup cornstarch
- 1 cup icing sugar (powdered sugar)
- 3 cups all-purpose flour

## Instructions:

1. Preheat your oven to 385°F (196°C).
2. In a large mixing bowl, cream the soft butter until it's smooth and creamy.
3. Sift the cornstarch and icing sugar into the bowl with the butter. Mix until well combined.
4. Gradually add the all-purpose flour to the mixture. Continue to mix until a smooth and cohesive dough forms. You can use a stand mixer or mix by hand.
5. Lightly flour a clean surface or parchment paper and roll out the shortbread dough to your desired thickness. Traditionally, shortbread is about ¼ to ½ inch thick.
6. Use cookie cutters to cut the dough into your preferred shapes. You can use round shapes, squares, or any other cookie cutter you like.
7. Place the cutout cookies on a baking sheet lined with parchment paper, leaving a little space between each.
8. Prick each cookie with a fork to create the traditional shortbread pattern.
9. Bake in the preheated oven for about 20-25 minutes or until the edges of the cookies start to turn golden brown. The baking time may vary slightly depending on your oven and the thickness of the cookies.
10. Remove the shortbread cookies from the oven and allow them to cool on a wire rack.
11. Once cooled, your shortbread cookies are ready to enjoy! They are buttery, crumbly, and perfect with a cup of tea or coffee.

Store any leftover cookies in an airtight container to keep them fresh.

Enjoy your homemade shortbread cookies!

**FOR DIABETICS:** not suggested.

# Lydia's Russian Borscht

## Ingredients:

- Salt and pepper (to taste)
- 10 potatoes
- 2 carrots
- 2 beets
- 4-5 cups cabbage (shredded)
- 1/4 onion (finely chopped)
- 1/4 cup butter
- Canned tomatoes (to taste)
- 1 cup heavy cream
- Fresh dill (for garnish)

## Instructions:

1. Prepare the Vegetables:
   - Peel the potatoes, carrots, and beets. Cut them into small, uniform pieces. This will ensure even cooking.
2. Sauté the Onions:
   - In a large soup pot, melt the butter over medium heat.
   - Add the finely chopped onions and sauté until they become translucent and fragrant.

3. Add the Root Vegetables:
   - Add the prepared potatoes, carrots, and beets to the pot.
   - Season with salt and pepper to taste.
4. Cook the Vegetables:
   - Pour in enough water to cover the vegetables.
   - Simmer over medium heat until the root vegetables are tender. This may take around 20-30 minutes, depending on the size of your vegetable pieces.
5. Incorporate the Cabbage:
   - Once the root vegetables are tender, add the shredded cabbage to the pot.
   - Continue to simmer until the cabbage is soft and wilted, usually about 10-15 minutes.
6. Add Canned Tomatoes:
   - Add canned tomatoes to taste for that characteristic deep red color and a hint of tanginess.
   - The amount of tomatoes you use can vary depending on your preference.
7. Finish with Cream:
   - Pour in the heavy cream to add richness and creaminess to the borscht.
   - Stir well to combine. Adjust the thickness with more cream or water if needed.
8. Adjust Seasoning:
   - Taste the borscht and adjust the seasoning with additional salt and pepper if necessary. Be mindful not to over-salt; you can always add more later.
9. Serve:
   - Ladle the hot borscht into bowls.
   - Garnish each serving with fresh dill, which adds a delightful herbaceous flavor and a burst of green color.

**FOR DIABETICS:** enjoy!

# Aunt Iris's Borscht

My Dad's Sister

## Ingredients:

- 1 cabbage, finely chopped (divide into two portions)
- 1 can tomatoes
- 1/2 cup peas
- 1 cup carrots, chopped
- 2 beets, cut in half
- 3-4 potatoes, diced
- 4 whole potatoes (to be used later)
- 1 cup water
- 1/4 lb butter
- Milk or cream for mashing potatoes

## Instructions:

1. In a large pot, combine one portion of the finely chopped cabbage, canned tomatoes, peas, chopped carrots, beets, diced potatoes, and water.
2. Place the whole potatoes in the soup.
3. Simmer the soup until the vegetables are cooked and tender. This may take some time as you want the flavors to meld together.
4. In a separate frying pan, sauté the other portion of finely chopped cabbage in butter until it becomes tender and caramelized.
5. Once the whole potatoes in the soup are cooked, remove them from the pot.
6. In a separate bowl, mash the whole potatoes with milk or cream until you get a creamy consistency. This will thicken the soup.
7. Add the sautéed cabbage to the soup, followed by the mashed potatoes. Stir everything together and continue simmering until the soup is ready to eat.
8. Taste and adjust the seasoning, adding more salt and pepper if needed.

9. Serve your homemade borscht hot, garnished with a dollop of sour cream if you like, and enjoy your comforting and nutritious soup!

**FOR DIABETICS**: enjoy!

# Aunt Iris's Homemade Pizza

## Ingredients:

*For the Pizza Dough:*

- 2 and 1/2 cups all-purpose flour
- 2 teaspoons active dry yeast or 1 pkg
- ½ teaspoon sugar
- ¼ teaspoon salt
- 1 cup warm water (110°F/43°C)
- ½ -1 tablespoons olive oil
- Cornmeal for sprinkling

*For the Pizza Toppings:*

- Tomato sauce or pizza sauce
- Shredded mozzarella cheese
- Your choice of toppings (e.g., pepperoni, sliced bell peppers, sliced olives, mushrooms, onions, etc.)

## Instructions:

*For the Pizza Dough:*

1. In a small bowl, combine the warm water and sugar. Sprinkle the yeast on top. Let it sit for about 5-10 minutes or until it becomes frothy and bubbly.
2. In a large mixing bowl, combine the flour and salt. Make a well in the center and pour in the yeast mixture and olive oil.
3. Mix the dough until it comes together. If it's too sticky, add a little more flour; if it's too dry, add a bit more water.

4. Knead the dough for about 5-8 minutes until it's smooth and elastic.
5. Form the dough into a ball and place it in a lightly oiled bowl. Cover it with a clean kitchen towel or plastic wrap and let it rise in a warm, draft-free place for about 20-30 minutes or until it has doubled in size.
6. To Assemble and Bake the Pizza:
   - Preheat your oven to 425°F (218.33°C) or as high as it will go, and place a pizza stone or an inverted baking sheet on the middle rack.
   - Lightly grease 2 pizza pans and sprinkle cornmeal.
   - Divide the dough into half.
7. On a floured surface, roll out the pizza dough into your desired shape and thickness.
8. Carefully transfer the rolled-out dough onto a piece of parchment paper.
9. Spread a layer of tomato sauce or pizza sauce over the dough, leaving a small border for the crust.
10. Sprinkle a generous amount of shredded mozzarella cheese over the sauce.
11. Add your choice of pizza toppings. Be creative and use your favorite ingredients.
12. Top with Tex-Mex Cheese
13. Carefully slide the parchment paper with the pizza onto the preheated pizza stone or baking sheet in the oven.
14. Bake for about 10-18 minutes or until the crust is golden brown and the cheese is bubbly and lightly browned.
15. Carefully remove the pizza from the oven using oven mitts. Let it cool for a minute or two before slicing and serving.

Enjoy your homemade pizza! You can always adjust the toppings and flavors to your liking.

**FOR DIABETICS**: substitute for a cauliflower pizza shell or "ritzza pizza"

# Cousin Barb's Fish Batter

Aunt Iris's Daughter

## Ingredients:

- 1 cup all-purpose flour
- 1 teaspoon baking powder
- 1/2 teaspoon salt
- 1/4 teaspoon garlic powder
- A pinch of cayenne pepper (adjust to taste)
- 1 cup beer
- 1/2 cup water

## Instructions:

1. In a mixing bowl, combine the flour, baking powder, salt, garlic powder, and cayenne pepper.
2. Gradually add the beer and water to the dry ingredients, whisking continuously until you have a smooth batter. Adjust the amount of cayenne pepper to your desired level of spiciness.
3. Let the batter rest for about 10-15 minutes. This allows the ingredients to meld together and the batter to thicken slightly.
4. While the batter is resting, prepare your fish fillets or seafood of choice.
5. Heat your frying oil to 350-375°F (175-190°C) in a deep fryer or a large, deep skillet.
6. Dip each piece of fish or seafood into the batter, coating it evenly. Allow any excess batter to drip off.
7. Carefully place the battered fish into the hot oil and fry until golden brown and crispy, usually about 3-5 minutes, depending on the thickness of the fish. Be sure not to overcrowd the pan; fry in batches if needed.
8. Once the fish is cooked, remove it from the oil using a slotted spoon or tongs and place it on a plate lined with paper towels to drain any excess oil.
9. Serve your deliciously crispy fish with your favorite dipping sauces, such as tartar sauce or lemon wedges, and enjoy!

This batter works great for fish and seafood like cod, haddock, shrimp, and more. Adjust the seasonings to your taste and experiment with different types of fish for a variety of flavors.

**FOR DIABETICS:** not suggested.

# Cousin Geoff's Pig Roast

Aunt Iris's Son

Roasting a whole pig is a grand culinary adventure and often a communal event. Here's a basic recipe for roasting a whole pig:

## Ingredients:

1. **Whole Pig:** The size of the pig will depend on your gathering. Smaller pigs are easier to handle, but a larger pig will feed more people. Ensure it's cleaned, gutted, and properly prepared by your butcher.
2. **Seasoning Rub:** Create a rub using a combination of herbs, spices, and seasonings of your choice. Common ingredients include garlic, paprika, oregano, thyme, salt, pepper, and olive oil.
3. **Wood or Charcoal:** You'll need a lot of wood or charcoal for the fire, depending on your cooking method.

## Equipment:

- **Rotisserie Spit:** A large rotisserie spit is essential for cooking the pig. Make sure it's sturdy enough to hold the weight of the pig.
- **Fire Pit or Grill:** You'll need a fire pit or large grill to support the rotisserie.
- **Thermometer:** A meat thermometer is crucial for monitoring the internal temperature of the pig.

## Instructions:

1. Preparation:
   - Prepare your pig by cleaning it thoroughly. Remove any hair, debris, or excess fat.
   - Season the pig generously with the rub, both inside and outside. Be sure to get the seasoning into the cuts and crevices for maximum flavor.
   - Truss or secure the pig onto the rotisserie spit, ensuring it's balanced.

161

2. Fire Preparation:
   - Build a fire in your fire pit or grill. The fire should be large enough to create an even heat source.
   - Let the fire burn down to hot coals. You want a steady, even heat source rather than open flames.
   - Set up your rotisserie over the hot coals.
3. Cooking:
   - Place the pig on the rotisserie and start the rotation.
   - Maintain a consistent temperature around 225°F to 250°F (107°C to 121°C). This is low and slow cooking.
   - Cook the pig for several hours, depending on its size. Plan for about 4 to 6 hours per 100 pounds of pig.
   - Use a meat thermometer to check the internal temperature. The pork should reach 160°F (71°C) in the thickest part of the meat.
   - Rotate the pig regularly to ensure even cooking and browning. Baste it occasionally with a flavorful liquid like apple juice or a vinegar-based sauce.
4. Resting and Serving:
   - Once the pig reaches the desired temperature, remove it from the rotisserie and let it rest for about 20-30 minutes.
   - Carve and serve your roasted pig. It's a communal affair, and many people prefer to eat it straight from the grill.

Roasting a whole pig is a labor-intensive process that requires careful monitoring of the fire and temperature. have guests bring a potluck dish and add a dash of live music. It's a wonderful way to bring people together for a memorable feast!

**FOR DIABETICS:** enjoy!

# Ellie's Soy Dressing

The owner of the Princeton Castle

## Ingredients:

- 3 tablespoons soy sauce
- 2 tablespoons avocado oil (you can also use olive oil)
- Optional: A squeeze of fresh lemon juice for a citrusy twist

## Instructions:

1. Combine Ingredients: In a small bowl, whisk together the soy sauce and avocado oil until well combined. You can also add a squeeze of fresh lemon juice for a bit of acidity and brightness.
2. Taste and Adjust: Taste the dressing and adjust the flavors as needed. If you'd like it to be saltier, add more soy sauce. For a richer flavor, add more avocado oil. Adjust to your personal preference.
3. Serve: Drizzle the soy dressing over your spinach salad or other green salads just before serving. Toss the salad to ensure the dressing is evenly distributed.
4. Enjoy: Enjoy your salad with the delicious soy dressing as a flavor enhancer!

**FOR DIABETICS:** enjoy!

# Aunt Diane's Pickled Eggs

My mom's older sister

## Ingredients:

- 6-8 large eggs
- 1 cup white vinegar
- 1 cup water
- 1/2 cup sugar
- 1 teaspoon salt
- 4-5 cloves garlic, peeled and crushed
- 1 small red (or white) onion, thinly sliced
- 1 teaspoon black peppercorns (optional)
- 1 teaspoon crushed red pepper flakes (optional)

## Instructions:

1. Start by hard-boiling the eggs. Place the eggs in a saucepan and cover them with cold water. Bring the water to a boil over high heat, then reduce the heat to medium-low and let the eggs simmer for about 10-12 minutes.
2. Drain the eggs and transfer them to a bowl of ice water to cool completely. Once cooled, peel the eggs and set them aside.
3. In a separate saucepan, combine the white vinegar, water, sugar, and salt. Bring this mixture to a boil, stirring until the sugar and salt are fully dissolved. Remove it from the heat and let it cool slightly.
4. In a clean, sterilized glass jar or container with a tight-fitting lid, layer the hard-boiled eggs, sliced red onions, crushed garlic, and optional black peppercorns and red pepper flakes.
5. Pour the slightly cooled vinegar mixture over the eggs and onions in the jar, ensuring that all the ingredients are fully submerged.
6. Seal the jar with a lid and refrigerate it for at least 24 hours to allow the flavors to meld. For the best taste, wait 2-3 days before consuming the pickled eggs.

7. Serve the pickled eggs as a delicious snack, appetizer, or side dish.

These pickled eggs with garlic and sliced red onions will have a tangy and slightly sweet flavor with a hint of garlic and onion.

**FOR DIABETICS**: enjoy!

# Aunt Diane's Pineapple Delight

## Ingredients:

- ¾ package of mini marshmallows
- 1 can of crushed pineapple, drained
- 1 cup of milk
- 1 ½ cups of graham wafer crumbs
- 1 cup of whipping cream

## Instructions:

1. **Dissolve Marshmallows:** Start by dissolving the mini marshmallows in a double boiler. To do this, place the marshmallows in the top part of the double boiler and gently heat them over simmering water. Stir occasionally until the marshmallows are completely melted. This will create a smooth marshmallow mixture. Once melted, remove it from the heat and allow it to cool.
2. **Whip Cream:** While the marshmallow mixture is cooling, whip the whipping cream until stiff peaks form. You can use a hand mixer or a stand mixer for this step. Be sure not to over-whip the cream, as it can become too stiff.
3. **Combine Ingredients:** Once the marshmallow mixture has cooled and the whipped cream is ready, gently fold the drained crushed pineapple into the marshmallow mixture. Then, fold in the whipped cream. Be gentle to maintain the light and fluffy texture.
4. **Layer with Graham Wafers:** Line a pan with graham wafer crumbs, reserving some for the top. You can use a 9x9-inch square pan or a similar-sized dish.
5. Pour Mixture: Pour the pineapple, marshmallow, and whipped cream mixture over the graham wafer crumbs in the pan. Spread it evenly.
6. **Top with Crumbs:** Sprinkle the remaining graham wafer crumbs over the top of the mixture to create a crumbly crust-like layer.
7. **Chill:** Cover the pan with plastic wrap or aluminum foil and refrigerate the Pineapple Delight for at least a few hours or

overnight. This allows the dessert to set and the flavors to meld together.

8. **Serve:** When you're ready to serve, cut the Pineapple Delight into squares or slices and enjoy your delicious dessert!

# OR

## Ingredients:

For the Crust:

- 1 1/2 cups graham cracker crumbs
- 1/2 cup unsalted butter, melted
- 1/4 cup granulated sugar

For the Filling:

- 8 oz cream cheese, softened
- 1 cup powdered sugar
- 8 oz whipped topping (like Cool Whip)
- 1 can (20 oz) crushed pineapple, drained
- 1/2 cup chopped pecans or walnuts (optional)

For the Topping:

- Additional whipped topping
- Maraschino cherries for garnish

## Instructions:

1. Prepare the Crust:
   - In a mixing bowl, combine the graham cracker crumbs, melted butter, and granulated sugar. Mix until the crumbs are evenly coated with butter.
   - Press the mixture into the bottom of a 9x13-inch serving dish to create the crust.
2. Prepare the Filling:

- In another mixing bowl, beat the softened cream cheese until it's smooth and creamy.
- Gradually add the powdered sugar and mix until well combined.
- Fold in the whipped topping until the mixture is light and fluffy.
- Gently fold in the drained crushed pineapple and chopped nuts, if using.

3. Assemble the Dessert:
    - Spread the cream cheese and pineapple mixture evenly over the graham cracker crust.
4. Chill and Serve:
    - Refrigerate the dessert for at least 2 hours or until it's set.
5. Serve:
    - Before serving, top the dessert with an additional layer of whipped topping.
    - Garnish with maraschino cherries.

**FOR DIABETICS**: not suggested.

# Aunt Diane's Rice Crispy Squares

## Ingredients:

- 3 tablespoons unsalted butter
- 1 package (10 ounces) marshmallows (about 40 marshmallows)
- 6 cups Rice Krispies cereal

## Instructions:

1. Prep the Pan:

- Grease a 9x13-inch baking pan or a similar-sized dish. You can also line it with parchment paper for easy removal.

2. Melt the Butter:

- In a large saucepan, melt the butter over low heat.

3. Add Marshmallows:

- Add the marshmallows to the melted butter and stir continuously until the marshmallows are completely melted, and the mixture is smooth. This should take about 3-4 minutes.

4. Combine with Cereal:

- Remove the saucepan from the heat.
- Add the Rice Krispies cereal to the melted marshmallow mixture. Stir until the cereal is evenly coated with the marshmallow mixture. You can use a buttered spatula to help with this step.

5. Press into Pan:

- Transfer the mixture into the prepared greased or lined pan.
- Use a buttered spatula or a piece of parchment paper to press the mixture firmly and evenly into the pan. Be sure to press down gently to avoid crushing the cereal too much.

6. Cool and Cut:

- Allow the Rice Krispie mixture to cool and set for about 30 minutes to an hour. It should become firm and easy to cut.
- Once it's cooled and set, use a sharp knife to cut the mixture into squares or rectangles.

7. Serve:

- Carefully remove the Rice Krispie Treats from the pan if you lined it with parchment paper, and place them on a serving platter.
- Serve and enjoy!

Rice Krispie Treats are best when they're fresh, but you can store any leftovers in an airtight container for a few days. If you'd like to add some variety, consider mixing in chocolate chips, M&M's, nuts, or other additions when you add the cereal to the marshmallow mixture.

**FOR DIABETICS**: not suggested

# Cousin Tricia's Japanese Salad

Aunt Diane's youngest daughter

## Ingredients:

- 1 small head of cabbage, shredded
- 3 cups bean sprouts
- 4 green onions, thinly sliced
- ½ cup slivered almonds
- 2 tablespoons sesame seeds
- ½ cup mushrooms, thinly sliced
- 1 package of Ichiban noodles (ramen noodles), crushed and dried

For the Sauce:

- ½ cup salad oil (vegetable or canola oil)
- ¼ cup vinegar (rice vinegar or white vinegar)
- 2 tablespoons soy sauce
- 1 tablespoon sugar
- Pepper to taste
- Ichiban spice from the package of ramen noodles

## Instructions:

1. Preheat your oven to 350°F (175°C).
2. Spread the slivered almonds and sesame seeds on a baking sheet and toast them in the preheated oven for 8-10 minutes or until they turn golden brown. Keep an eye on them to prevent burning. Once toasted, remove them from the oven and let them cool.
3. In a large mixing bowl, combine the shredded cabbage, bean sprouts, sliced green onions, toasted almonds, sesame seeds, sliced mushrooms, and crushed dried Ichiban noodles.
4. In a separate bowl, whisk together the salad oil, vinegar, soy sauce, sugar, pepper, and the Ichiban spice from the ramen noodle package. This will be your dressing.

5.  Pour the dressing over the salad mixture and toss everything together until well combined. Make sure the dressing evenly coats the salad ingredients.
6.  Let the salad sit in the refrigerator for at least 30 minutes to allow the flavors to meld and the noodles to soften slightly.
7.  Before serving, give the salad another good toss to ensure the dressing is well distributed.
8.  Serve your Japanese salad as a side dish or a light meal.

This Japanese salad is crisp, crunchy, and full of flavor. It's a wonderful combination of textures and tastes, and the toasted almonds and sesame seeds add a delightful nutty flavor. Enjoy!

**FOR DIABETICS**: For a diabetic-friendly version of Japanese salad that doesn't include noodles, you can replace the noodles with low-carb or low-glycemic index alternatives. Here are some options:

- **Zucchini Noodles** (Zoodles): Spiralized zucchini makes an excellent low-carb replacement for traditional noodles. They have a similar texture and can absorb the flavors of the salad dressing.
- **Shirataki Noodles**: Shirataki noodles are made from konjac yam and are very low in carbohydrates and calories. They are virtually carb-free and have a neutral flavor, making them a good choice for diabetics.
- **Cucumber Noodles**: Thinly sliced or spiralized cucumbers can add a refreshing crunch to your salad without adding many carbs.
- **Riced Cauliflower**: Finely grated or riced cauliflower can be used to mimic the texture of noodles. Simply blanch or sauté the cauliflower rice briefly before adding it to the salad.

# Aunt Camille's Perogies

Another one of my mom's three sisters, the youngest

## Ingredients:

- Frozen perogies (your choice of flavor)
- Sour cream
- Bacon slices
- 1 medium onion, finely chopped
- Butter for frying
- Salt and pepper to taste
- Chopped fresh parsley (optional, for garnish)

## Instructions:

1. Cook the Bacon:

- In a large skillet, cook the bacon slices over medium heat until they are crispy. Remove the bacon from the skillet and place it on paper towels to drain. Once cooled, crumble the bacon into small pieces. Set it aside.

2. Sauté the Onion:

- In the same skillet with the bacon drippings, add the finely chopped onion. Sauté the onion over medium heat until it becomes soft and translucent, about 5 minutes. Remove the sautéed onions from the skillet and set them aside.

3. Boil the Perogies:

- Follow the package instructions to boil the frozen perogies. Typically, you'll need to bring a large pot of salted water to a boil, add the perogies, and cook them until they float to the surface, which usually takes about 3-5 minutes. Drain them well.

4. Optional: Fry the Perogies:

- In the same skillet you used for bacon and onions, melt a few tablespoons of butter over medium heat.
- Add the boiled perogies to the skillet and fry them until they are golden brown on both sides. This should take about 2-3 minutes per side.

5. Serve:

- Serve the fried perogies on a plate.
- Top them with the sautéed onions and crumbled bacon.
- Add a dollop of sour cream on top.
- Season with salt and pepper to taste.
- Garnish with chopped fresh parsley if desired.

OR

## HOMEMADE PEROGIES

### Ingredients:

For the Dough:

- 2 cups all-purpose flour
- 1/2 teaspoon salt
- 1 large egg
- 1/2 cup sour cream
- 1/4 cup unsalted butter, softened
- 1/4 cup water (or as needed)

For the Filling:

- 2 cups mashed potatoes (about 4 medium-sized potatoes, boiled and mashed)

- 1 cup grated cheddar cheese
- 1/2 small onion, finely chopped (optional)
- Salt and pepper to taste

For Cooking:

- Water for boiling
- Butter or oil for frying (optional)
- Sour cream for serving (optional)

## Instructions:

1. Prepare the Dough:
   - In a large mixing bowl, combine the flour and salt.
   - In a separate bowl, whisk together the egg, sour cream, and softened butter.
   - Add the wet mixture to the dry mixture and stir until it starts to come together.
     - Gradually add water a tablespoon at a time, and knead the dough until it's smooth and not sticky. You may not need all the water, so add it sparingly.
2. Make the Filling:
   - In a bowl, combine the mashed potatoes, grated cheddar cheese, finely chopped onion (if using), and season with salt and pepper to taste. Mix well.
3. Roll Out the Dough:
   - On a lightly floured surface, roll out the dough to about 1/8-inch thickness.
4. Cut and Fill:
   - Use a round cutter (approximately 3 inches in diameter) to cut circles from the rolled-out dough.
   - Place a small spoonful of the potato and cheese filling in the center of each dough circle.
5. Seal the Perogies:
   - Fold the dough over the filling to create a half-moon shape.
   - Press the edges together firmly to seal the perogies. You can use a fork to crimp the edges for a decorative touch.
6. Boil the Perogies:

- Bring a large pot of salted water to a boil.
- Carefully add the perogies to the boiling water and cook for about 3-5 minutes or until they float to the surface. Be gentle when adding them to avoid sticking.

7. Optional Frying:
    - After boiling, you can pan-fry the perogies in butter or oil until they are golden brown on both sides for added flavor and texture.

8. Serve:
    - Serve the perogies hot with sour cream on the side for dipping.

Enjoy your homemade perogies! You can customize the filling to your liking, including using ingredients like sautéed onions, bacon, or mushrooms.

**FOR DIABETICS**: not suggested.

# Uncle Al's Bannock

Aunt Camille's
Husband

## Ingredients:

- 4 cups flour
- 3 tablespoons sugar
- 3 tablespoons baking powder
- 1/2 cup lard or shortening
- Raisins (as many as you like)
- Water

## Instructions:

1. In a mixing bowl, combine the flour, sugar, and baking powder. Mix these dry ingredients together.
2. Cut in the lard or shortening until the mixture resembles coarse crumbs. You can do this by using a pastry cutter or your fingers.
3. Add raisins to the mixture. You can add as many as you like, depending on your preference.
4. Gradually add water to the mixture, a little at a time, and stir until you have a dough that holds together. Be cautious not to add too much water; you want the dough to be firm but pliable.
5. Once the dough is ready, divide it into portions and shape each portion into a long, thin strip, like a snake or a rope.
6. Wrap the dough strips around sticks or skewers, leaving some space between the coils to allow for even cooking.
7. Cook the Bannock over an open fire, turning them occasionally to ensure even cooking. They should cook for about 20-25 minutes or until they are golden brown and cooked through.

8. Carefully remove the Bannock from the sticks, and they are ready to enjoy!

These Bannock sticks make a fun and delicious outdoor treat, perfect for a snowshoe hike or any outdoor adventure. Just be sure to exercise caution when working with an open flame. Enjoy your nummy Bannack!

I still remember like it was yesterday: he took us kids for a snowshoe hike and then made a fire. Wrapped some dough around a stick and cooked it over the fire.

Nummy!

**FOR DIABETICS:** Not suggested.

# Aunt Phyllis's Seven Layer Salad

Uncle Denis's Wife (one of my mom's two brothers, the oldest)

## Ingredients:

For the Salad Layers:

- 6 cups torn lettuce (iceberg or Romaine)
- 1 cup chopped red bell pepper
- 1 cup chopped cucumber
- 1 cup chopped red onion
- 1 cup frozen peas, thawed
- 1 cup shredded cheddar cheese
- 6-8 slices of cooked and crumbled bacon

For the Dressing:

- 2 cups mayonnaise
- 2 tablespoons sugar
- 1 tablespoon white vinegar
- Salt and pepper to taste

## Instructions:

1. Start by preparing the dressing. In a bowl, combine the mayonnaise, sugar, white vinegar, salt, and pepper. Mix well until the sugar has dissolved and the dressing is smooth. Taste and adjust the seasoning if needed. Set the dressing aside.
2. In a large glass or trifle dish or a clear salad bowl, begin layering the salad ingredients in the following order:
   - First Layer: Place the torn lettuce on the bottom as the base layer.
   - Second Layer: Add the chopped red bell pepper.
   - Third Layer: Sprinkle the chopped cucumber evenly over the peppers.
   - Fourth Layer: Spread the chopped red onion.
   - Fifth Layer: Distribute the thawed frozen peas.
   - Sixth Layer: Sprinkle the shredded cheddar cheese.
   - Seventh Layer: Finish with the crumbled bacon on top.
3. After creating the seven layers, pour the dressing evenly over the top of the salad, making sure to cover all the ingredients.
4. Cover the salad with plastic wrap or a lid and refrigerate for at least 2 hours, or overnight if possible. Chilling allows the flavors to meld and the salad to become crisp and delicious.
5. Just before serving, you can garnish the top with additional bacon bits, cheese, or fresh parsley, if desired.
6. Use a large spoon or serving utensil to scoop out portions, making sure to get all the layers. Serve chilled.

Seven Layer Salad is a visually appealing and tasty dish that's great for potlucks and picnics. It's customizable, so feel free to add or omit ingredients to suit your taste. Enjoy!

**FOR DIABETICS**: enjoy!

# Aunt Phyllis's Broccoli Salad

## Ingredients:

For the Salad:

- 5 cups fresh broccoli florets (about 1 head of broccoli)
- 3 green onion, finely chopped
- 1/2 cup grapes (green or red), raisins, or dried cranberries
- 3/4 cup toasted almonds or chopped nuts (e.g., sunflower seeds, walnuts)
- 1/2 cup shredded cheddar cheese (optional)

For the Dressing:

- 1 cup mayonnaise
- 1/3 cup sugar (adjust to taste)
- 1 tablespoon balsamic vinegar
- Salt and pepper to taste
- (I like adding bacon bits)

## Instructions:

1. Start by preparing the dressing. In a small bowl, whisk together the mayonnaise, sugar, vinegar, salt, and pepper. Taste the dressing and adjust the sugar, salt, and pepper to your preference. Set the dressing aside.
2. In a large salad bowl, combine the fresh broccoli florets, finely chopped green onion, grapes, raisins or dried cranberries, almonds or chopped nuts, and shredded cheddar cheese (if using).
3. Pour the prepared dressing over the salad ingredients. Use a spatula or spoon to gently toss everything together until the broccoli and other ingredients are well coated with the dressing.
4. Cover the bowl with plastic wrap or a lid and refrigerate for at least an hour before serving. Chilling allows the flavors to meld, and the salad becomes more flavorful.
5. Before serving, give the salad a final toss to redistribute the dressing. You can also garnish with additional nuts, seeds, or cheese if desired.

This classic broccoli salad is customizable, so feel free to add other ingredients like crispy bacon bits or diced red bell pepper for extra flavor and crunch. It's a great side dish for picnics, barbecues, or any gathering. Enjoy!

**FOR DIABETICS**: use alternate sugar.

# Aunt Phyllis's Taco Salad

## Ingredients:

For the Salad:

- 1 lb ground beef or ground turkey
- 4 green onions, chopped
- 1 packet taco seasoning mix
- 2 tbsp soy sauce
- 1 tbsp chili powder
- 14oz can tomato sauce
- 1 head of iceberg lettuce, shredded
- 1 cup cherry tomatoes, halved
- 1 cup shredded medium cheddar cheese
- Salt and pepper to taste
- Optional: 1 cup canned kidney beans, drained and rinsed
- Optional: 1 cup canned corn kernels, drained
- Optional: 1/2 red onion, finely chopped
- Optional: 1/4 cup black olives, sliced
- Optional: 1 avocado, diced

For the Dressing:

- 1/2 cup sour cream
- 1/2 cup ranch dressing

For Garnish:

- Tortilla chips or strips

## Instructions:

1. In a large skillet, brown the ground beef or turkey over medium heat until fully cooked. Drain any excess fat.
2. Add chopped green onions to the cooked meat and sauté for a few minutes until they become tender.
3. Stir in the taco seasoning mix, soy sauce, chili powder, and tomato sauce. Simmer the mixture for about 20 minutes,

allowing the flavors to meld together. Remove from heat and let it cool.

4. In a large salad bowl, combine the shredded iceberg lettuce, halved cherry tomatoes, shredded cheddar cheese, and any optional ingredients you'd like to include, such as kidney beans, corn, red onion, black olives, and diced avocado.
5. Once the meat mixture has cooled, toss it with the salad ingredients in the bowl. Make sure everything is well combined.
6. In a separate small bowl, prepare the dressing by mixing together the sour cream and ranch dressing until smooth.
7. Drizzle the dressing over the taco salad and gently toss to coat all the ingredients with the dressing.
8. Season the salad with salt and pepper to taste.
9. Garnish the taco salad with tortilla chips or strips for added crunch and texture.
10. Serve the taco salad immediately, and enjoy your flavorful and satisfying meal!

**FOR DIABETICS:** enjoy!.

# Jack's Ceasar Salad Dressing

Husband of a Friend of Pops (Nick)

## Ingredients:

- 1 egg
- 4-5 cloves of garlic, minced
- 1 tin (about 2 ounces) of anchovies, drained
- 2 tablespoons Dijon mustard
- 2 tablespoons lemon juice
- 1 dash of Tabasco sauce (adjust to taste)
- 3 dashes of Worcestershire sauce (adjust to taste)
- 1 cup olive oil

## Instructions:

1. **Prepare Ingredients:** Begin by mincing the garlic cloves and draining the anchovies if they aren't already. You can use a food processor or a blender for this recipe.
2. **Blend Anchovies and Garlic:** In a food processor or blender, combine the minced garlic and anchovies. Pulse or blend until they form a smooth paste.
3. **Add Mustard and Lemon Juice:** Add the Dijon mustard and lemon juice to the garlic and anchovy mixture. Blend again until well combined.
4. **Incorporate Hot Sauce and Worcestershire Sauce:** Add the Tabasco sauce and Worcestershire sauce to the mixture. You can adjust the amount to your preferred level of spiciness and tanginess.
5. **Add the Egg:** Crack the egg into the mixture. Make sure to use a fresh, clean, and pasteurized egg since this recipe uses a raw egg. Blend everything together until smooth.
6. **Slowly Drizzle in Olive Oil:** With the food processor or blender running on low, slowly drizzle in the olive oil. Continue blending until the dressing emulsifies and thickens. This process should take a couple of minutes. Scrape down the sides of the container if needed to ensure everything is well combined.

7. **Taste and Adjust:** Taste the dressing and adjust the seasoning to your preference. You can add more lemon juice, Worcestershire sauce, or hot sauce as needed.
8. **Serve:** Transfer the Caesar salad dressing to an airtight container or jar. Store it in the refrigerator until you're ready to use it. The dressing can be kept for a few days.

When you're ready to enjoy your Caesar salad, toss the dressing with fresh romaine lettuce, croutons, and grated Parmesan cheese. You can also add grilled chicken or shrimp for a heartier version. Enjoy your homemade Caesar salad!

**FOR DIABETICS**: enjoy!

# Jack's Potato Salad

## Ingredients:

- 9 hard-boiled eggs, peeled and mashed
- 3/4 cup Hellmann's mayonnaise
- 3/4 teaspoon curry powder
- Salt and pepper to taste
- 1/3 cup chopped shallots (or substitute with garlic or onions)
- 2 pounds yellow/golden Yukon potatoes (yellow-fleshed potatoes)
- 1 to 4 golden apples, cored and chopped

## Instructions:

1. **Boil the Potatoes:** Place the Yukon potatoes in a large pot and cover them with water. Add a pinch of salt. Bring the water to a boil, then reduce the heat to a simmer. Cook the potatoes until they are fork-tender but not falling apart. This will usually take about 15-20 minutes, depending on the size of the potatoes.

2. **Cool and Peel Potatoes:** Drain the potatoes and let them cool to room temperature. Once cooled, peel the potatoes and cut them into bite-sized cubes.

3. **Prepare the Eggs:** While the potatoes are cooling, hard-boil the eggs. Place the eggs in a pot of cold water and bring to a boil. Once boiling, reduce the heat to a simmer and cook for about 9-12 minutes. Drain the eggs and transfer them to a bowl of ice water to cool. Once cooled, peel the eggs and mash them in a separate bowl.

4. **Make the Dressing:** In a large mixing bowl, combine the mashed eggs, Hellmann's mayonnaise, curry powder, salt, pepper, and chopped shallots. Mix everything together until well combined. Adjust the seasoning to taste.

5. **Combine Potatoes and Apples:** Gently fold the cooled and cubed potatoes and chopped apples into the egg and mayonnaise mixture. Be careful not to mash the potatoes; you want them to stay in chunks.

6. **Chill and Serve:** Cover the potato salad and refrigerate for at least 1-2 hours before serving. This allows the flavors to meld together. Before serving, you can garnish with additional chopped fresh herbs, such as parsley or chives, if desired.

**FOR DIABETICS**: not suggested.

# Jack's Yorkshire Pudding

## Ingredients:

- 4 eggs
- 200ml whole milk
- 1 ¼ cups sifted flour
- Pinch of salt (1/8 tsp)

## Instructions:

1. Preheat your oven to 370°F (190°C).
2. Pour about 1 centimeter of sunflower oil into the top three molds. Tip the muffin tin and let the oil flow into all the molds, ensuring it reaches the bottom molds.
3. Place muffin tin on a flat tray and place in the oven for 15 minutes.
4. While the oil is heating, crack the eggs into a mixing bowl and whisk them until well-beaten.

5. Add the whole milk to the beaten eggs and continue to whisk, ensuring they are fully combined.
6. Sift the flour into the egg and milk mixture to avoid any lumps.
7. Add a pinch of salt (approximately 1/8 teaspoon) for seasoning.
8. Mix the ingredients thoroughly until you have a smooth batter with no lumps. The batter should have a pouring consistency.
9. Optional: once the oil in the muffin tin is hot, you can add a teaspoon of beef dripping into each mold for added flavor.
10. Remove the tin from the oven and carefully scoop the egg mixture into each hot oil-filled muffin space. The oil should be sizzling when the batter is added.
11. Then, place the muffin tin with the batter-filled molds back into the oven.
12. Allow the Yorkshire puddings to bake for 25-30 minutes. It's essential NOT TO OPEN THE OVEN DOOR or peek during this time to ensure they rise properly.
13. After the specified time, your Yorkshire puddings should be beautifully risen and golden brown.
14. Remove the Yorkshire puddings from the oven and serve them immediately as a delicious side dish for roast meats, gravy, or other accompaniments.

Enjoy your homemade Jack's Yorkshire Pudding, a classic British dish that adds a delightful touch to your roast dinners or special occasions. The key is to have patience and avoid opening the oven door while they're baking to achieve the perfect rise and texture.

**FOR DIABETICS:** Not suggested.

# Jack's Chicken

## Ingredients:

For Breading:

- 4 eggs
- 2-3 cups all-purpose flour
- Oil for frying (e.g., vegetable oil)

For Chicken:

- Chicken wings (e.g., Costco chicken wings)

For Sweet and Sour Sauce:

- 1 cup granulated sugar
- 3 tablespoons China Lily soy sauce
- 1/2 cup white vinegar (Hintz brand)

## Instructions:

Breading and Frying:

1. Beat the eggs in a bowl to create an egg wash.
2. Place the flour in a separate bowl for dredging.
3. Heat oil in a pan or deep fryer. To test if the oil is hot enough, you can sprinkle a tiny amount of water into the oil. If it sizzles and pops, the oil is ready (around 350-375°F or 175-190°C).
4. Take each chicken wing, dip it into the beaten eggs, and then coat it in flour, making sure to knock off any excess flour.
5. Carefully place the breaded chicken wings into the hot oil and fry them until they are golden brown and crispy. This usually takes about 5-7 minutes, but the exact time may vary depending on the size of the wings and the temperature of the oil.

6. Remove the fried chicken wings from the oil and let them drain on paper towels to remove excess oil.

Sweet and Sour Sauce:

7. In a separate saucepan, combine the sugar, China Lily soy sauce, and white vinegar.
8. Using a whisk, mix the ingredients together until the sugar is completely dissolved.
9. Heat the sauce over medium heat until it comes to a simmer. Let it simmer for a few minutes, stirring occasionally, until the sauce thickens slightly. It should have a sweet and sour flavor.

Baking with Sauce:

10. Preheat your oven to 350°F (175°C).
11. Place the fried chicken wings in a baking dish.
12. Pour the sweet and sour sauce over the chicken wings, making sure they are evenly coated.
13. Bake the chicken wings in the preheated oven for 20-30 minutes, basting them with the sauce after the first 10 minutes of baking.
14. Remove the chicken from the oven when they are heated through and the sauce has caramelized slightly.
15. Serve the Jack's Chicken with Sweet and Sour Sauce as a delicious snack or main dish.

**FOR DIABETICS:** use alternative sugar and flour.

# Big Connie's Chocolate Chip Cookies

I am little Connie in my family. She was Uncle Brad's 1st wife.

## Ingredients:

- 1 cup (2 sticks) unsalted butter, softened
- 1/2 cup granulated sugar
- 1 cup brown sugar, packed
- 2 large eggs
- 2 teaspoons pure vanilla extract
- 2 cups all-purpose flour
- ½ cup flaked oats
- 1 teaspoon baking soda
- 1/2 teaspoon salt
- 2 cups semi-sweet chocolate chips

## Instructions:

1.  Preheat your oven to 375°F (190°C).
2.  In a large mixing bowl, cream together the softened butter, granulated sugar, and brown sugar until the mixture is light and fluffy.
3.  Add the eggs one at a time, beating well after each addition. Stir in the vanilla extract.
4.  In a separate bowl, whisk together the all-purpose flour, baking soda, flaked oats, and salt.
5.  Gradually add the dry ingredients to the wet ingredients, mixing until just combined. Be careful not to overmix.
6.  Gently fold in the semi-sweet chocolate chips until they are evenly distributed throughout the cookie dough.
7.  Drop rounded tablespoons of cookie dough onto ungreased baking sheets, spacing them about 2 inches apart.
8.  Bake in the preheated oven for 9-11 minutes or until the edges are golden brown, but the centers are still soft.
9.  Remove the cookies from the oven and allow them to cool on the baking sheets for a few minutes before transferring them to wire racks to cool completely.
10. Once cooled, store the chocolate chip cookies in an airtight container to keep them fresh.

Enjoy your homemade Chocolate Chip Cookies with a glass of milk or your favorite beverage!

**FOR DIABETICS:** Not suggested.

# Ben's Wife's Banana Muffins

I worked for Ben when I was in my early twenties.

## Ingredients:

- 1 cup butter
- 1 cup sugar
- 2 beaten eggs
- 3 ripe bananas, mashed
- 1/2 cup buttermilk or sour milk (To make sour milk, add 3/4 tablespoon of lemon juice to 1/2 cup of milk)
- 2 teaspoons vanilla extract
- 2 1/2 cups all-purpose flour
- 2 1/2 teaspoons baking powder
- 2 teaspoons baking soda
- 1/2 teaspoon salt
- Optional: Chocolate chips and/or nuts

## Instructions:

1. Preheat the Oven:
   - Preheat your oven to 400°F (200°C). Prepare a muffin tin by lining it with paper liners or greasing it.
2. Cream Butter and Sugar:

- In a mixing bowl, cream together the softened butter and sugar until it's light and fluffy.
3. Add Eggs:
    - Beat the eggs and add them to the butter-sugar mixture. Mix well.
4. Mash Bananas:
    - Peel and mash the ripe bananas. You can use a fork to do this. Add the mashed bananas to the mixture and combine.
5. Mix in Buttermilk and Vanilla:
    - Stir in the buttermilk (or sour milk) and vanilla extract until well incorporated.
6. Combine Dry Ingredients:
    - In a separate bowl, whisk together the flour, baking powder, baking soda, and salt.
7. Blend Dry Ingredients:
    - Gradually add the dry ingredients to the wet mixture. Stir until just combined; do not overmix. If you're adding chocolate chips or nuts, gently fold them into the batter.
8. Fill Muffin Cups:
    - Fill each muffin cup about two-thirds full with the muffin batter. You can use a spoon or an ice cream scoop for even portions.
9. Bake:
    - Place the muffin tin in the preheated oven and bake for about 20 minutes or until a toothpick or cake tester inserted into the center of a muffin comes out clean.
10. Cool:
    - Allow the banana muffins to cool in the muffin tin for a few minutes, then transfer them to a wire rack to cool completely.

Once your banana muffins are completely cooled, they are ready to enjoy. These muffins are moist, flavorful, and perfect for breakfast or as a snack. Feel free to customize them with your favorite additions, like chocolate chips or nuts.

**FOR DIABETICS:** Not suggested.

# Aunt Lynn's Salmon

A good friend of my
mom's.

## Ingredients:

- Fresh salmon fillet
  (catch or buy)
- Mayonnaise
- Lemon slices
- Onion slices
- Salt and pepper to taste

## Instructions:

1. Preheat the Oven:
   - Preheat your oven to 350°F (175°C) to prepare for
     baking.
2. Prepare the Salmon:
   - If you've caught the salmon, make sure it's properly
     cleaned and filleted. If you've bought it, ensure it's fresh
     and cleaned.
3. Season the Inside:
   - Lay the salmon fillet skin-side down on a clean surface.
   - Spread a layer of mayonnaise on the inside of the salmon
     skin. The mayo will help keep the salmon moist while
     cooking.
   - Place slices of lemon and onion on top of the mayo layer.
     These will infuse the salmon with flavor.
   - Season the inside of the salmon with salt and pepper to
     taste.
4. Fold and Close:
   - Carefully fold the salmon fillet over, encasing the lemon,
     onion, and seasoning inside. You want to create a
     "salmon pocket" with the skin on the outside.
   - If the salmon doesn't stay closed on its own, you can use
     kitchen twine or toothpicks to secure it.
5. Mayo on the Outside:

- Now, spread a thin layer of mayonnaise on the outside of the salmon skin. This will help the skin crisp up and seal in the flavors.

6. Wrap in Foil:
   - Place the salmon, skin-side down, in the center of a sheet of aluminum foil large enough to completely wrap it.
   - Carefully fold the foil over the salmon, sealing the edges to create a well-sealed packet.

7. Baking:
   - Place the foil-wrapped salmon on a baking sheet or in an ovenproof dish.
   - Bake the salmon in the preheated oven for about 1 hour or until it's cooked through. Cooking times can vary depending on the thickness of the salmon fillet, so you can check for doneness by inserting a fork or knife into the thickest part of the fillet. If it flakes easily and is opaque in the center, it's done.

8. Serve:
   - Carefully unwrap the foil packet and transfer the salmon to a serving platter.
   - You can garnish it with additional fresh herbs, lemon slices, or onions if desired.

Your baked salmon should be tender, flavorful, and perfectly cooked. Enjoy your meal!

## Cleaning and filleting

Cleaning and filleting a freshly caught salmon can be a bit involved, but with the right tools and some practice, it can be a rewarding process. Here's a general guide on how to clean and fillet a salmon:

Tools You'll Need:

- Fillet knife
- Cutting board
- Gutting scoop or spoon
- Clean water source or bucket
- Disposable gloves (optional)
- A cooler filled with ice to store the fillets

## Instructions:

1. Safety First:
   - If you're new to cleaning fish, consider wearing disposable gloves to protect your hands from scales and potential fish odors.
2. Prepare a Clean Work Area:
   - Start by setting up a clean, well-lit area for filleting. Lay down a clean cutting board, and ensure you have access to a water source for rinsing the fish and your hands.
3. Remove Scales:
   - Hold the salmon securely by the tail.
   - Use a fillet knife or scaler to scrape off the scales from the tail to the head. Be sure to remove all scales for a smoother filleting process.
4. Gut the Fish:
   - Lay the salmon on its side.
   - Insert a gutting scoop or spoon into the anus of the salmon and gently scoop out the innards. Be careful not to puncture the intestines, as this can release strong odors and contaminate the meat.
   - Rinse the salmon thoroughly to remove any remaining blood or debris.
5. Remove the Head (Optional):
   - If you prefer to fillet the salmon without the head, use your fillet knife to make a horizontal cut just behind the gills. Remove the head by cutting through the spine.
   - Some people prefer to keep the head attached for presentation purposes or to utilize the cheek meat.
6. Start Filleting:
   - Lay the cleaned salmon on its side on the cutting board.
   - Begin the filleting process by making a vertical cut just behind the pectoral fin (near the head) down to the spine.
   - Angle your knife slightly toward the spine as you cut to maximize the meat yield.
7. Follow the Backbone:
   - Continue filleting by following the spine, making long, smooth cuts down the length of the fish.
   - Gradually angle your knife to follow the ribcage and remove the fillet.

- Be cautious around the ribcage to avoid damaging the meat.
8. Flip and Repeat:
    - Flip the salmon over and repeat the filleting process on the other side.
9. Check for Remaining Bones:
    - Once both fillets are removed, carefully run your fingers along each fillet to detect and remove any remaining pin bones.
10. Rinse and Store:
    - Rinse the fillets with clean water to remove any loose scales, blood, or impurities.
    - Place the fillets in a cooler filled with ice to keep them fresh.

Not to remember, that filleting a fish, especially a salmon, takes practice to perfect. It's a skill that many anglers and seafood enthusiasts develop over time. If you're unsure about the process, you can also seek guidance from experienced fishermen or fishmongers.

**FOR DIABETICS:** enjoy!

# Ken's Crab

Aunt Lynn's second husband.

## Ingredients:

- Fresh crab
- Water (ideally seawater, but freshwater works)
- Juice of 2 lemons
- 2 bay leaves
- 1 teaspoon salt

## Instructions:

1. Prepare the Crab:
   - Ensure the crab is thoroughly cleaned and its top shell (carapace) and guts are removed.
2. Boil Water:
   - Fill a large pot with enough water to submerge the crab fully. If you have access to seawater, use it; otherwise, freshwater is fine.

- Place the pot on the stove and turn on the heat.
3. Season the Water:
   - Squeeze the juice of 2 lemons into the boiling water.
   - Add 2 bay leaves and 1 teaspoon of salt to the water.
4. Boil the Crab:
   - Carefully lower the cleaned crab into the boiling water. You can use tongs or a long spoon to do this.
5. Cook for 4 Minutes:
   - Allow the crab to boil in the seasoned water for about 4 minutes. Cooking times can vary slightly depending on the crab's size, so you may need to adjust accordingly.
   - Look for the crab's shell to turn a bright orange-red color, which indicates it's done cooking.
6. Remove and Serve:
   - Carefully lift the crab out of the boiling water. You can use tongs or a slotted spoon.
   - Let the crab drain briefly to remove excess water.
   - Your boiled crab is now ready to be enjoyed. Serve it as-is or with your favorite dipping sauce (melted butter).

These are general instructions for boiling crab, and cooking times may vary depending on the crab's size and species. Enjoy your delicious freshly boiled crab!

Even though there is a professional way to catch, clean, and cook crab before eating it. Watching Nick (hubby) dive down and get the crab then give it to Ken was fascinating. Who took the crab by its back and smashed its belly on a hard corn of the boat. Next, he swished it in the sea water, then place it in the pot filled with fresh seawater that he just scooped from the ocean. Wow, crab has never tasted so yummy!

**FOR DIABETICS:** enjoy!

# Uncle Rick's Ribs

Grammy's brother-n-law

## Ingredients:

- 1 cup chili sauce
- 1 cup President's Choice Beer & Chipotle BBQ sauce (or your favorite BBQ sauce with chipotle flavor)
- 1/2 cup brown sugar
- 1/4 cup lemon juice
- 1 teaspoon mustard powder
- 3-4 pounds of pork ribs, cut into serving-sized portions (3-4 ribs per portion)
- Aluminum foil

## Instructions:

1. **Prepare the Sauce:** In a mixing bowl, combine the chili sauce, BBQ sauce, brown sugar, lemon juice, and mustard powder. Mix well until all the ingredients are incorporated. This sauce will be used to coat and marinate the ribs.
2. **Coat and Marinate the Ribs:** Take the cut ribs and generously coat them with the sauce mixture. Make sure all

sides are coated evenly. You can use a brush or your hands for this. Once the ribs are coated, place them in a large zip-top bag or a covered container. Pour any remaining sauce over the ribs. Seal the bag or container and refrigerate the ribs to marinate overnight. Marinating the ribs will infuse them with flavor and tenderize the meat.

3. **Preheat the Oven:** Remove the marinated ribs from the refrigerator about an hour before cooking to bring them to room temperature. Preheat your oven to 350°F (175°C).

4. **Wrap the Ribs:** Cut aluminum foil into pieces that are large enough to wrap each portion of ribs. Place each portion on a piece of foil and wrap it tightly, sealing the edges.

5. **Bake the Ribs:** Place the wrapped ribs on a baking sheet. Bake them in the preheated oven at 350°F for 1 hour. After the first hour, reduce the oven temperature to 275°F (135°C) and continue baking for another hour. This slow-cooking process will make the meat tender and flavorful.

6. **Check for Doneness:** After the second hour, carefully unwrap one of the rib portions. The meat should be tender and easily come away from the bone.

7. **Serve:** Serve the delicious chili and beer chipotle BBQ ribs hot with your favorite side dishes.

**FOR DIABETICS:** enjoy!

# Mary's Soups

When I was going to open Merlin's at the Castle in Princton, Mary created these recipes for me.

# Cream of Mushroom Soup

## Ingredients:

- 3 quarts (12 cups) water
- 1/4 cup butter
- 3/4 pound mushrooms, sliced
- 1/4 cup finely diced onion
- 1/2 stalk celery, finely chopped
- 3 tablespoons liquid bouillon (chicken)
- 6 tablespoons dry bouillon (chicken)
- 1/4 teaspoon baking soda
- 1/2 cup canned milk

- 1 tablespoon grated carrot
- 6 tablespoons of a thickening agent (such as cornstarch) mixed in 3/4 cup water

## Instructions:

1. **Saute Mushrooms:** In a 4-quart pot, sauté the sliced mushrooms in the butter until they become tender.
2. **Add Water and Bring to Boil:** Add the 3 quarts of water to the pot with sautéed mushrooms and bring it to a boil.
3. **Add Onion, Celery, and Carrot:** Once the water is boiling, add the finely diced onion, finely chopped celery, and grated carrot to the pot. Bring it back to a boil.
4. **Add Chicken Bouillon:** Stir in both the liquid and dry chicken bouillon into the soup.
5. **Add Baking Soda:** Once the onion, celery, and carrot are cooked and tender, add the baking soda. This step is important to prevent the milk from curdling when you add it.
6. **Add Canned Milk:** Pour in the canned milk and stir to combine with the soup.
7. **Thicken the Soup**: In a separate bowl, mix 6 tablespoons of your chosen thickening agent (such as cornstarch) with 3/4 cup of water until it forms a smooth paste. Gradually add this mixture to the soup, stirring constantly.
8. **Gentle Boil and Remove from Heat:** Bring the soup to a gentle boil while continuing to stir. Once it reaches the desired thickness, remove it from heat.

This recipe makes a large batch of Cream of Mushroom soup. You can store any leftovers in the refrigerator and reheat it when you're ready to enjoy it. Cream of Mushroom soup is a versatile base for various recipes, or you can simply savor it on its own.

**FOR DIABETICS:** enjoy!

# Cream of Broccoli Soup

## Ingredients:

- 3 quarts (12 cups) water
- 3/4 cup celery, finely minced
- 3/4 cup onion, finely minced
- 2 heads of fresh broccoli (or 1 kg frozen), cut up
- 2 tablespoons finely grated carrot
- 3 tablespoons liquid bouillon (chicken)
- 2 tablespoons dry bouillon (chicken)
- 1/2 cup canned milk
- 1/4 cup Cheese Whiz
- 1/2 teaspoon salt
- 1/4 teaspoon baking soda (to prevent curdling)
- 6 tablespoons cornstarch stirred into 1/2 cup water (for thickening)

## Instructions:

1. **Bring Water to a Boil:** In a large 1-gallon pot, bring the salted water to a boil.
2. **Add Vegetables:** Add the finely minced celery, finely minced onion, and cut-up broccoli to the boiling water. Simmer until the vegetables are tender.
3. **Add Grated Carrot:** Stir in the finely grated carrot.
4. **Add Chicken Bouillon:** Add both the liquid and dry chicken bouillon to the soup, stirring to combine.
5. **Mash Broccoli:** Use a potato masher to further break down the broccoli in the soup.
6. **Add Cheese Whiz:** Stir in the Cheese Whiz until it is completely blended into the soup.
7. **Incorporate Baking Soda:** Add the baking soda and stir well. This will help prevent curdling when you add the milk.
8. **Add Canned Milk:** Pour in the canned milk and continue to stir until the soup gently boils.
9. **Thicken the Soup:** In a separate bowl, mix the cornstarch with 1/2 cup of water until it forms a smooth paste. Gradually add this cornstarch mixture to the soup, stirring constantly.

10. **Remove from Heat:** Once the soup reaches the desired thickness, remove it from the heat.

This recipe yields a generous amount of Cream of Broccoli Soup. You can store any leftovers in the refrigerator and reheat it when you're ready to enjoy it. It's a delightful way to savor the flavors of broccoli in a creamy soup.

**FOR DIABETICS:** enjoy!

# Chicken Soup

## Ingredients:

- 3 quarts (12 cups) water
- 1 large cooked chicken breast, cubed
- 3/4 cup celery, chopped
- 3/4 cup onion, finely minced
- 4 tablespoons liquid bouillon (chicken)
- 1 tablespoon dry bouillon (chicken)
- 1/2 cup peas
- 1 cup diced carrot
- 1/2 teaspoon salt

## Instructions:

1. **Bring Water to a Boil:** In a large pot, bring the 3 quarts of water to a boil.
2. **Add Chicken:** Once the water is boiling, add the cubed chicken breast to the pot.
3. **Add Vegetables:** Stir in the chopped celery, finely minced onion, peas, and diced carrot.
4. **Add Bouillon:** Add both the liquid and dry chicken bouillon to the soup, stirring to combine.
5. **Season with Salt:** Add the salt to taste.
6. **Simmer:** Reduce the heat to a simmer and let the soup cook until the vegetables are tender, typically about 20-30 minutes.

7. **Additional Options:**
   - For Chicken Rice Soup: Add 1/4 cup of rice to the simmering soup and cook until the rice is tender.
   - For Chicken Noodle Soup: Add 1/2 cup of broken fettuccine noodles to the simmering soup and cook until the noodles are soft.
8. **Serve:** Once the soup is cooked to your desired consistency and the flavors have melded together, it's ready to be served.

This recipe is versatile, and you can adjust the ingredients and seasonings to suit your preferences.

**FOR DIABETICS:** enjoy!

# Garden Vegetable Soup

## Ingredients:

- 2 large stalks of celery, chopped
- 3/4 cup chopped green pepper
- 1 cup green beans
- 1/2 cup chopped mushrooms
- 1 cup diced onion
- 1 1/2 cups carrot, quartered and sliced
- 1 1/2 cups zucchini, quartered and sliced
- 14 oz can of diced tomatoes
- 3/4 teaspoon fennel
- 1/2 teaspoon basil
- 4 tablespoons vegetable bouillon
- 3 quarts water
- 1/2 teaspoon salt (or to taste)
- 1/4 teaspoon pepper

## Instructions:

1. **Bring Water to a Boil:** In a large pot, bring 3 quarts of water to a boil.

2. **Add Vegetables:** Once the water is boiling, add all the chopped vegetables and the canned diced tomatoes to the pot.
3. **Return to Boil:** Return the mixture to a boil.
4. **Season:** Stir in the fennel, basil, vegetable bouillon, salt, and pepper. Adjust the seasonings to taste.
5. **Simmer:** Reduce the heat to a simmer and let the soup cook until the vegetables are very tender, typically about 30-40 minutes.
6. **Serve:** Once the vegetables are tender and the flavors have melded together, your Garden Vegetable Soup is ready to be served.

**FOR DIABETICS:** enjoy!

# Beef Barley Soup

## Ingredients:

- 1 pound steak, cubed small
- 3 quarts water
- 1 1/2 stalks celery, diced
- 2 1/2 cups diced carrots
- 1 1/2 cups diced onion
- 1/3 cup barley
- 6 tablespoons beef base
- 3/4 cup peas (frozen)
- 1 1/2 cups diced potatoes
- 2 tablespoons olive oil

## Instructions:

1. **Sauté the Beef:** In a large pot, heat 2 tablespoons of olive oil over medium-high heat. Add the cubed steak and sauté until browned on all sides.
2. **Boil Water:** In a separate 1-gallon pot, bring 3 quarts of water to a boil.

3. **Add Vegetables and Barley:** Once the water is boiling, add the celery, carrots, diced onion, barley, diced potatoes, and peas to the pot.
4. **Simmer:** Allow the soup to simmer until the vegetables and barley are tender. This will typically take about 30-40 minutes.
5. **Add Sautéed Beef:** Once the vegetables and barley are tender, add the sautéed beef to the soup.
6. **Stir in Beef Base:** Stir in the beef base to flavor the soup. Adjust the seasoning to taste, if needed.
7. **Simmer Again:** Simmer the soup for an additional 15 minutes to let all the flavors meld together.
8. **Serve:** Your Beef Barley Soup is ready to be served. Enjoy this hearty and comforting soup on a chilly day.

**FOR DIABETICS:** enjoy!

# Turkey Soup

## Ingredients:

- Leftover turkey carcass with some meat on it (picked from previous meal)
- 4-5 quarts water
- 2 stalks celery, chopped
- 1 cup diced onion
- 1 1/2 cups diced carrot
- 3/4 cup frozen peas
- 2 cups diced potatoes
- 2 teaspoons salt (adjust to taste)
- 2-3 tablespoons chicken bouillon (optional, for extra flavor)
- Leftover turkey meat, diced

## Instructions:

1. **Prepare the Turkey Carcass:** Pick any remaining meat from the turkey carcass and set it aside. You will use this meat in the soup.
2. **Boil the Turkey Bones:** In a large Dutch oven or pot, place the turkey carcass with any leftover meat and cover it with 4-5 quarts of water. Bring it to a boil. Allow the bones to boil for about 2 hours. This will create a flavorful turkey broth.
3. **Strain the Broth:** After boiling, strain the liquid to remove the bones and return the strained liquid (the turkey broth) to the pot. Discard the bones.
4. **Add Vegetables:** To the turkey broth, add chopped celery, diced onion, diced carrots, frozen peas, diced potatoes, and salt. You can also add any leftover turkey gravy at this stage for extra flavor.
5. **Simmer:** Bring the mixture to a boil, then reduce the heat to a simmer. Allow it to simmer until the vegetables are tender. This usually takes about 20-30 minutes.
6. **Add Diced Turkey:** Dice any leftover turkey meat and add it to the pot. Simmer until the turkey is heated through.
7. **Adjust Seasoning:** Taste the soup and adjust the seasoning as needed. If you feel the broth lacks flavor, you can add 2-3 tablespoons of chicken bouillon for an extra boost.
8. **Serve:** Ladle the turkey soup into bowls and serve it hot. Optionally, you can garnish it with fresh herbs like parsley or thyme.

**FOR DIABETICS:** enjoy!

# Pork and Beans

## Ingredients:

- 1 lb white beans (soaked overnight)
- 1 lb uncooked pork, cubed
- 2 tsp liquid smoke
- 1 medium-large onion, diced
- 1/2 cup celery, chopped

213

- 1 cup sugar
- 1 tbsp white vinegar
- 1 tbsp dry mustard
- 2 cups ketchup
- 1/2 cup molasses
- 1/4 cup Tony Roma's hickory BBQ sauce
- 1/2 tsp salt
- Optional: Pork chops to cook with the dish

## Instructions:

1. Soak and Cook Beans:
   - Begin by soaking the white beans in water overnight. After soaking, drain the beans, and then boil them in a large pot with fresh water until they become soft, which typically takes about 2 hours. Drain the beans, but be sure to reserve 3 cups of the cooking liquid. Set this liquid aside.
2. Marinade Pork:
   - While the beans are cooking, marinade the cubed pork in 2 teaspoons of liquid smoke for about 10 minutes.
3. Prepare Vegetables:
   - Dice the onion and chop the celery.
4. Combine Ingredients:
   - In a large roasting pan, combine the cooked beans, marinated pork, diced onion, and chopped celery. Stir these ingredients together.
5. Prepare Sauce:
   - In a separate bowl, prepare the sauce by mixing together 1 cup of sugar, 1 tablespoon of white vinegar, 1 tablespoon of dry mustard, 2 cups of ketchup, 1/2 cup of molasses, 1/4 cup of Tony Roma's hickory BBQ sauce, and 1/2 teaspoon of salt.
6. Combine Sauce and Ingredients:
   - Pour the prepared sauce over the bean and pork mixture in the roasting pan. Stir everything together until well combined.
7. Optional Pork Chops:
   - If you want to include pork chops, you can place them on top of the mixture in the roasting pan.

8. Bake:
   - Cover the roasting pan and bake at 325°F (163°C) for 2 1/2 to 3 hours. This will allow the flavors to meld and the pork and beans to become tender.
9. Serve:
   - Once baked, remove the dish from the oven. If you added pork chops, they should be cooked through. Serve the pork and beans hot.

**FOR DIABETICS:** use sugar alternative.

# My Husband's Recipes

## Nicholas (Nick / Pops)

Ah, the memories of youthful exuberance and the early days of our marriage fill my heart with a mix of amusement and reflection. As a new wife, I embarked on a culinary adventure that would teach me valuable lessons about love, partnership, and the art of cooking. Little did I know that my journey  would be sprinkled with moments of regret and realization.

One recipe stands out in this culinary chronicle—the infamous lasagna. What possessed me to believe that I could master it with ease, I'll never quite fathom. As I clumsily navigated the kitchen, attempting to recreate a beloved dish, I quickly learned that practice truly makes perfect. The layers of pasta, sauce, and cheese were a canvas upon which I discovered the true meaning of perseverance and culinary determination.

In hindsight, I wonder if I should have let my husband have that lasagna, embracing his culinary prowess and granting him the title of "Master of Lasagna." Perhaps I should have relished in the thought of him taking charge of this delectable creation, a dish that he could craft effortlessly while I marveled at his skill.

But alas, my determination and stubbornness prevailed, and I managed to conquer the lasagna recipe after countless trials and tribulations. In doing so, I unintentionally claimed that culinary territory for myself, sealing my fate as the designated lasagna chef.

However, there is a silver lining to this tale of culinary conquest. My husband found his culinary domain in a realm that brought joy to our mornings—breakfast. With finesse and flair, he embraced the art of breakfast-making. His famous waffles, omelets that melted in the mouth, and his mastery over bacon (oh, the heavenly aroma!) became his signature dishes. In the realm of breakfast, he reigned supreme, a culinary maestro that I gladly ceded to.

Looking back, I shake my head at my younger self, wondering why I was so eager to take on every culinary challenge that came my way. As time has passed, I've come to realize that true culinary harmony isn't about conquering every dish; it's about embracing each other's strengths and passions.

So, as I continue to create lasagnas and marvel at my husband's breakfast delights, I recognize that our culinary journey is a reflection of our partnership. It's a tapestry woven with laughter, learning, and a deep appreciation for each other's unique gifts. While I may have claimed the lasagna as my own, I am grateful for the lessons it taught me about humility, sharing, and the art of finding balance in the kitchen and in life.

# Eggs Beni

## Ingredients:

- Eggs (1 for each muffin half)
- English muffins
- Slices of ham or Canadian back bacon
- Hollandaise sauce (follow the instructions below or use your preferred recipe)
- Fresh parsley for garnish

Hollandaise Sauce Ingredients (or use a packet):

- 3 large egg yolks
- 1 tablespoon lemon juice
- 1/2 cup unsalted butter, melted
- Pinch of cayenne pepper
- Pinch of salt

Hollandaise Sauce Instructions:

1. In a blender, combine the egg yolks, lemon juice, cayenne pepper, and salt. Blend for a few seconds until well mixed.
2. While the blender is running, slowly drizzle in the melted butter in a steady stream. Continue blending until the sauce thickens and becomes smooth, which should take about 20-30 seconds.
3. Taste the hollandaise sauce and adjust the seasoning if necessary. If it's too thick, you can add a little warm water and blend again to reach your desired consistency.
4. Keep the hollandaise sauce warm until you're ready to use it. You can place it in a heatproof bowl over a pot of simmering water (double boiler) or use a thermos to maintain its temperature.

## Assembly **Instructions**:

5.  Begin by poaching the eggs. To poach an egg, bring a pot of water to a simmer. Add a splash of white vinegar to the simmering water (this helps the egg whites coagulate nicely). Gently crack an egg into a small bowl and then slide it into the simmering water. Poach the egg for about 3-4 minutes for a runny yolk or longer if you prefer it more cooked. Use a slotted spoon to carefully remove the poached egg from the water and drain it on a paper towel.
6.  While the eggs are poaching, toast the English muffins until they're golden brown.
7.  Place a slice of ham or Canadian back bacon on each toasted English muffin half.
8.  Once the poached eggs are ready, carefully place one on top of each slice of ham or Canadian bacon.
9.  Spoon hollandaise sauce generously over each poached egg. You can adjust the amount according to your taste.
10. Garnish each Eggs Benedict with a sprinkle of fresh parsley for a touch of color and freshness.
11. Serve your Eggs Benedict immediately while they're warm, and enjoy this classic and indulgent breakfast or brunch dish.
12. Eggs Benedict is a delightful combination of flavors and textures that makes for a perfect brunch option. The creamy hollandaise sauce complements the perfectly poached egg and the savory ham or bacon, all nestled on a toasted English muffin.

**FOR DIABETICS:** See Bun/Muffin Alternatives

# Waffles

## Ingredients:

- 2 cups all-purpose flour
- 2 tablespoons sugar
- 1 tablespoon baking powder
- 1/2 teaspoon salt
- 2 large eggs
- 1 3/4 cups milk

- 1/2 cup vegetable oil       or melted butter
- 1 teaspoon vanilla extract

## Instructions:

1. Preheat the Waffle Iron:
   - Plug in your waffle iron and preheat it according to the manufacturer's instructions.
2. Mix Dry Ingredients:
   - In a large mixing bowl, whisk together the flour, sugar, baking powder, and salt.
3. Prepare Wet Ingredients:
   - In another bowl, beat the eggs and then add the milk, vegetable oil (or melted butter), and vanilla extract. Mix until well combined.
4. Combine Wet and Dry Ingredients:
   - Pour the wet ingredients into the bowl with the dry ingredients. Stir until just combined; a few lumps are okay. Do not overmix; overmixing can make the waffles tough.
5. Grease the Waffle Iron:
   - Lightly grease the waffle iron with non-stick cooking spray or a small amount of melted butter.
6. Cook the Waffles:

- Pour an appropriate amount of waffle batter (usually about 1/2 to 3/4 cup, depending on your waffle iron's size) onto the preheated waffle iron.
- Close the waffle iron and cook until the waffles are golden brown and crisp. The cooking time may vary depending on your waffle iron, but it's typically around 4-5 minutes.

7. Serve:
   - Carefully remove the cooked waffles from the iron using a fork or spatula.
   - Serve the waffles immediately with your favorite toppings, such as maple syrup, fresh berries, whipped cream, or a dusting of powdered sugar.

**FOR DIABETICS:** not suggested. See almond pancakes.

# Pancakes

## Ingredients:

- 1 ½ cup all-purpose flour
- 1 tablespoon sugar
- 3 1/2 teaspoons baking powder
- 1/2 teaspoon baking soda
- 1/2 teaspoon salt
- 1 1/2 cup buttermilk (or substitute with 1 cup milk mixed with 1 tablespoon white vinegar or lemon juice. Let it sit for 5 minutes)
- 1 large egg
- 3 tablespoons unsalted butter, melted
- Cooking spray or additional butter for greasing the skillet
- Optional: Add-ins like chocolate chips, blueberries, or sliced bananas

## Instructions:

1. In a large mixing bowl, whisk together the flour, sugar, baking powder, baking soda, and salt.
2. In a separate bowl, whisk together the buttermilk, egg, and melted butter.
3. Pour the wet ingredients into the dry ingredients and stir until just combined. Be careful not to overmix; a few lumps are okay. If you're adding any optional ingredients like chocolate chips or fruit, fold them into the batter gently.
4. Preheat a non-stick skillet or griddle over medium-high heat. You can lightly grease it with cooking spray or a small amount of butter.
5. Using a ladle or measuring cup, pour the pancake batter onto the hot skillet to make your desired pancake size (usually about 1/4 to 1/3 cup of batter per pancake).
6. Cook until you see bubbles forming on the surface of the pancake and the edges look set, usually about 2-3 minutes.

7. Flip the pancake with a spatula and cook the other side for an additional 1-2 minutes or until it's golden brown and cooked through.
8. Remove the pancake from the skillet and keep warm. You can place them on a plate in a warm oven (about 200°F or 95°C) until all the pancakes are ready.
9. Continue making pancakes with the remaining batter, greasing the skillet as needed.
10. Serve your pancakes with your favorite toppings, such as maple syrup, fresh fruit, whipped cream, or a dollop of yogurt.

**FOR DIABETICS:** not suggested. See almond pancakes.

# Traditional Lasagna

## Ingredients:

- 9 lasagna noodles (oven-ready or regular, cooked according to package instructions)
- 1 pound ground beef or Italian sausage
- 1 onion, finely chopped
- 3 cloves garlic, minced
- 1 (28-ounce) can crushed tomatoes
- 1 (6-ounce) can tomato paste
- 2 (14.5-ounce) cans diced tomatoes
- 2 teaspoons sugar
- 2 teaspoons dried basil
- 1 teaspoon dried oregano
- Salt and pepper to taste
- 2 cups ricotta cheese
- 1 egg
- 3 cups shredded mozzarella cheese
- 1 cup grated Parmesan cheese
- Fresh basil or parsley for garnish (optional)

## Instructions:

1. Preheat your oven to 375°F (190°C).
2. In a large skillet or saucepan, cook the ground beef or Italian sausage over medium heat until browned. Break it into small pieces as it cooks. Drain any excess fat.
3. Add the finely chopped onion and minced garlic to the skillet with the cooked meat. Sauté for about 5 minutes until the onions are translucent.
4. Stir in the crushed tomatoes, tomato paste, diced tomatoes, sugar, basil, oregano, salt, and pepper. Simmer the sauce for about 15-20 minutes, allowing the flavors to meld and the sauce to thicken. Adjust seasoning as needed.
5. In a separate bowl, mix the ricotta cheese and the egg until well combined.
6. Spread a thin layer of the meat sauce on the bottom of a 9x13-inch baking dish.
7. Place three lasagna noodles on top of the sauce in the dish.

8. Spread half of the ricotta cheese mixture over the noodles, followed by a portion of the mozzarella and Parmesan cheese.
9. Add another layer of meat sauce over the cheese.
10. Repeat the layers: noodles, remaining ricotta mixture, more mozzarella and Parmesan, and meat sauce.
11. Finish with a final layer of noodles, the remaining meat sauce, and the remaining mozzarella and Parmesan cheese.
12. Cover the baking dish with aluminum foil and bake in the preheated oven for about 25 minutes.
13. Remove the foil and continue to bake for an additional 10-15 minutes or until the cheese is melted and bubbling and the lasagna is hot throughout.
14. Let the lasagna rest for about 10 minutes before slicing and serving.
15. Garnish with fresh basil or parsley if desired.

Enjoy your delicious homemade traditional lasagna! It's a hearty and comforting Italian classic that's perfect for family dinners and gatherings.

**FOR DIABETICS:** not suggested. See the zucchini lasagna.

# Wor Won Ton Soup

## Ingredients:

For the Wontons:

- 1/2 pound ground pork
- 1/2 pound small shrimp, peeled, deveined, and finely chopped
- 2 green onions, finely chopped
- 1 clove garlic, minced
- 1/2 teaspoon ginger, minced
- 1 tablespoon soy sauce
- 1 teaspoon sesame oil
- 1 package wonton wrappers (about 50 wrappers)
- Water (for sealing wontons)

For the Soup:

- 8 cups chicken or vegetable broth
- 1 cup sliced bok choy or Chinese cabbage
- 1 cup sliced mushrooms (shiitake or button mushrooms work well)
- 1/2 cup sliced bamboo shoots
- 1/2 cup sliced water chestnuts
- 1/2 cup baby corn, halved
- 1/2 cup sliced carrots
- 1/2 cup snow peas, trimmed
- 1/2 cup sliced red bell pepper
- 1/2 cup sliced yellow bell pepper
- 1/2 cup sliced green bell pepper
- 2 tablespoons soy sauce
- 1 tablespoon oyster sauce (optional)
- Salt and white pepper to taste

## Instructions:

For the Wontons:

1. In a mixing bowl, combine the ground pork, chopped shrimp, green onions, minced garlic, minced ginger, soy sauce, and sesame oil. Mix until well combined.
2. Lay out a wonton wrapper on a clean, dry surface. Place about 1 teaspoon of the pork and shrimp mixture in the center of the wrapper.
3. Moisten the edges of the wonton wrapper with water. Fold it diagonally to create a triangle and press to seal, ensuring there are no air pockets.
4. Take the two opposite corners of the triangle and bring them together, sealing them with a dab of water to form a classic wonton shape.
5. Repeat the process with the remaining wonton wrappers and filling.

For the Soup:

1. In a large soup pot, bring the chicken or vegetable broth to a boil.
2. Add the sliced bok choy, mushrooms, bamboo shoots, water chestnuts, baby corn, carrots, snow peas, and bell peppers to the boiling broth. Let it simmer for about 5-7 minutes until the vegetables are tender but still crisp.
3. Stir in the soy sauce and oyster sauce (if using). Season with salt and white pepper to taste.
4. Carefully add the wontons to the simmering soup. Cook for an additional 5-7 minutes or until the wontons float to the surface and the filling is cooked through.
5. Once the wontons are cooked, the soup is ready to serve.
6. Ladle the hot soup into serving bowls, making sure each bowl gets a generous portion of wontons and vegetables.
7. Garnish with additional sliced green onions, if desired.
8. Serve the Wor Won Ton Soup hot and enjoy!

**FOR DIABETICS:** dumplings are not suggested.

# Seafood Chowder

## Ingredients:

- 1/4 cup butter
- 2 cups water
- 1/4 lb sliced bacon
- 1/2 onion, finely chopped
- 1 celery stalk, finely chopped
- 1 carrot, finely chopped
- 1 clove garlic, minced
- 2 tablespoons all-purpose flour
- 2 cups fish or seafood broth
- 3 cups diced potatoes
- 1/4 teaspoon curry powder
- 2 teaspoons fresh parsley, chopped
- Salt and pepper to taste
- 1-quart whole milk
- 1/2 cup heavy cream or evaporated milk
- 1/2 pound white fish fillets (such as cod or haddock), cut into bite-sized pieces
- 1/2 pound shrimp, peeled and deveined
- 1/2 pound scallops
- 1/2 pound lobster meat, 1" pieces
- Optional: 1/4 cup corn kernels (fresh or frozen)
- Optional: 1/4 cup peas (fresh or frozen)

## Instructions:

1. In a large soup pot, melt the butter over medium heat. Add the chopped onion, celery, carrots, and minced garlic. Sauté for about 5-7 minutes until the vegetables become soft and translucent.
2. Sprinkle the flour over the sautéed vegetables and stir well to coat. Cook for an additional 2-3 minutes, stirring constantly.
3. Gradually pour in the fish or seafood broth while continuing to stir. This will help prevent lumps from forming. Bring the mixture to a simmer.

4. Add the diced potatoes, parsley, salt, and pepper to the pot. Simmer for about 15-20 minutes or until the potatoes are tender.
5. Pour in the whole milk and heavy cream, stirring to combine. Allow the chowder to return to a simmer.
6. Gently add the fish, shrimp, scallops, corn kernels, and peas to the simmering chowder. Cook for another 5-7 minutes or until the seafood is opaque and cooked through.
7. Taste the chowder and adjust the seasoning with more salt and pepper if needed.
8. Ladle the hot seafood chowder into serving bowls, garnish with chopped fresh parsley, and serve immediately.
9. Optionally, serve with crusty bread or oyster crackers for dipping.

**FOR DIABETICS:** enjoy!

# Crab Melt Recipe

## Ingredients:

- 8 ounces lump crabmeat, drained and picked over for shells
- 1/4 cup mayonnaise
- 2 tablespoons grated Parmesan cheese
- 1 green onion, finely chopped
- 1/2 teaspoon Old Bay seasoning (optional)
- 1/2 teaspoon Dijon mustard (optional)
- Salt and pepper to taste
- 4 slices of your favorite bread (such as sourdough, wheat or white)
- 4 slices of Swiss or cheddar cheese
- Butter for spreading on the bread (optional)

## Instructions:

1. In a bowl, combine the lump crabmeat, mayonnaise, grated Parmesan cheese, chopped green onion, Old Bay seasoning, Dijon mustard, salt, and pepper. Mix until all the ingredients are well combined.
2. Preheat your oven's broiler.
3. Lay out the slices of bread and butter on one side of each slice (optional).
4. Place a scoop of the crab mixture onto the unbuttered side of each slice of bread.
5. Top the crab mixture with a slice of Swiss or cheddar cheese.
6. Place the prepared sandwiches on a baking sheet and put them under the broiler for 2-3 minutes or until the cheese is melted and bubbly and the crab mixture is heated through.
7. Remove from the oven and serve immediately.

# Tuna Melt Recipe

## Ingredients:

- 2 cans (5 ounces each) tuna, drained
- 1/4 cup mayonnaise
- 2 tablespoons finely chopped celery
- 2 tablespoons finely chopped red onion
- 1 tablespoon dill pickle relish (optional)
- Salt and pepper to taste
- 4 slices of your favorite bread (such as whole wheat or rye)
- 4 slices of cheddar or American cheese
- Butter for spreading on the bread (optional)

## Instructions:

1. In a bowl, combine the drained tuna, mayonnaise, chopped celery, chopped red onion, dill pickle relish (if using), salt, and pepper. Mix until everything is well combined.
2. Preheat your oven's broiler.
3. Lay out the slices of bread and butter on one side of each slice (optional).
4. Place a portion of the tuna mixture onto the unbuttered side of each slice of bread.
5. Top the tuna mixture with a slice of cheddar or American cheese.
6. Place the prepared sandwiches on a baking sheet and put them under the broiler for 2-3 minutes or until the cheese is melted and bubbly and the tuna mixture is heated through.
7. Remove from the oven and serve hot.

You can customize them to your taste by adding ingredients like sliced tomatoes, avocado, or pickles if you like. Enjoy your crab melt and tuna melt sandwiches!

**FOR DIABETICS:** Choose your bread wisely.

Why did the carpenter bring a sandwich to work?

Because he heard it was a construction site!

# My Recipes

## Dr. Constance (Connie / GiGi)

The journey of my culinary repertoire has been one of adaptation and transformation, mirroring the ever-changing dynamics of my family's preferences and the evolving landscape of health and well-being. As I navigate the tapestry of flavors, I find myself weaving a story that encompasses taste, love, and the pursuit of wholesome nourishment.

From the days of accommodating the likes and dislikes of my own little family to the present challenge of prioritizing health and wellness, my kitchen has been a canvas where creativity and consideration unite. Each chapter has brought its own set of discoveries, lessons, and transformations.

In the early years, my culinary creations were guided by the palates of my loved ones. I crafted meals that catered to their preferences, fostering a sense of unity and satisfaction around the dinner table. But as time moved forward, new considerations emerged, urging me to view food not just as a source of comfort but as a means to nourish and support well-being.

Long before it became a trend, I embarked on a path of innovation, exploring ways to merge taste with health-conscious choices. Lasagna noodles transformed into zucchini noodles, a subtle shift that brought both flavor and nutrient-density to the table. Pizza metamorphosed into "ritzza" pizza, a creative adaptation that embraced both taste and dietary needs. Spaghetti noodles gracefully bowed out to the arrival of spaghetti squash, offering a light and wholesome alternative.

The culinary landscape expanded further as cauliflower took on a new role as "cauliflower bread," and nut crackers became a staple that aligned with my evolving approach to nourishment. With each transformation, I discovered the art of embracing ingredients that celebrated both my culinary legacy and my commitment to well-being.

As I reflect on this journey, I realize that my kitchen has been a hub of experimentation, innovation, and love. It's a place where I've bridged the gap between tradition and modernity, crafting dishes that honor the past while embracing the future. This journey has been a testament to the versatility of ingredients and the power of adaptation.

In the realm of my kitchen, flavors have transformed, ingredients have evolved, and the very essence of my cooking has shifted to encompass a holistic approach to nourishment. With every recipe that underwent a makeover, I discovered that health and taste are not mutually exclusive—they can coexist harmoniously, creating a symphony of flavors that uplift both the body and the soul.

As I continue to explore the possibilities that my kitchen holds, I am reminded that the evolution of my culinary journey is a reflection of my own growth and the boundless potential that each meal possesses. With every dish I create, I embrace the legacy of taste, love, and innovation, weaving a story that celebrates both the past and the present in a tapestry of nourishment and well-being.

# Chai Tea

"Spice of Life Elixir"

## Ingredients:

- 1/8 tsp White Pepper
- ½ tsp Cinnamon
- ½ tsp Clove
- ½ tsp Cardamom
- ½ tsp Nutmeg
- 1 tsp Ginger
- 1 cup Powdered French Vanilla Creamer
- ½ tsp Allspice
- 1 cup Cane Sugar (optional)
- 1 cup Dry Milk Powder (optional)
- ¼ cup Honey Granules (optional)
- 1 Chai Tea packet to each cup you drink

## Instructions:

1. In a mixing bowl, combine the enchanting elements of 1/8 tsp of White Pepper, ½ tsp of Cinnamon, ½ tsp of Clove, ½ tsp of Cardamom, ½ tsp of Nutmeg, and 1 tsp of Ginger. These spices form the heart of your Spice of Life Elixir, infusing it with warmth and richness.
2. Add 1 cup of Powdered French Vanilla Creamer into the mixture, allowing the essence to intermingle with the spices, creating a symphony of flavors that dance on the palate.
3. Embrace the enchanting allure of ½ tsp of Allspice, adding a touch of complexity that awakens the senses and elevates the elixir's essence.
4. The choice is yours—add 1 cup of Cane Sugar to sweeten your elixir, granting it a gentle sweetness that encapsulates comfort and delight. Alternatively, you can choose to omit this ingredient if you prefer a less sweet blend.
5. If desired, incorporate 1 cup of Dry Milk Powder, allowing its velvety texture to enrich the elixir and create a harmonious fusion of flavors and creaminess.

6.  For an additional layer of sweetness and depth, consider adding ¼ cup of Honey Granules, infusing your elixir with the natural goodness of honey.
7.  Gently mix all the ingredients, ensuring that the spices are well distributed and the flavors harmoniously blended.
8.  As you whisk the ingredients, take a moment to appreciate the sensory symphony that unfolds—a tapestry of spices, creaminess, and sweetness that beckons you to savor the moment.
9.  Transfer the Spice of Life Elixir to an airtight container, preserving its captivating flavors for future enjoyment.
10. To indulge in the essence of this elixir, simply add a spoonful to your favorite hot beverage—be it coffee, 1 Chai Tea packet, another tea, or warm milk—and experience the magic of its spices and creamy embrace.

Note: This recipe is a canvas of possibility, allowing you to customize the sweetness and creaminess according to your preferences. Whether you choose to include cane sugar, dry milk powder, or honey granules, the result is a sensory elixir that warms the heart and nourishes the soul.

**FOR DIABETICS:** replace sugar with sugar alternative.

# Creamy Red Pepper Hummus Dip

Ingredients:

- 1 can of chickpeas, drained and rinsed
- 125 ml of Tahini
- ½ cup olive oil
- 2 tablespoons lemon juice
- 2 tablespoons white vinegar
- 2 cloves garlic
- ½ red pepper, roasted and peeled
- Salt and pepper, to taste
- 1/3 teaspoon dill
- Vegetable and onion spice, to taste
- Water, as needed for thickness

Instructions:

1. Start by roasting the red pepper. Place the red pepper on a baking sheet and roast it in the oven at 400°F (200°C) until the skin is charred and blistered. This usually takes about 20-25 minutes. Once roasted, carefully place the pepper in a bowl and cover it with a lid or plastic wrap to allow it to steam. After about 10 minutes, peel off the charred skin, remove the seeds, and chop the pepper into smaller pieces.
2. In a food processor, combine the drained and rinsed chickpeas, Tahini, olive oil, lemon juice, white vinegar, garlic cloves, and the roasted red pepper pieces.
3. Blend the ingredients until they start to form a smooth paste. If the mixture is too thick, you can gradually add water to achieve your desired consistency.
4. Add salt and pepper to taste, adjusting the seasoning as needed.
5. Sprinkle in the dill, vegetable, and onion spice, adjusting the quantities to suit your preferences.
6. Continue blending until the hummus reaches a creamy and velvety texture, ensuring all the flavors are well combined.

7. Taste the hummus and make any necessary adjustments to the seasonings, spices, or lemon juice to achieve the perfect balance of flavors.
8. Once the hummus is smooth and well-seasoned, transfer it to a serving bowl.
9. Drizzle a little extra olive oil over the top and garnish with a sprinkle of dill for an added visual and aromatic touch.
10. Serve your Creamy Red Pepper Hummus Dip with an array of dippable options such as fresh vegetables, pita bread, or whole-grain crackers.

Note: This hummus dip is a delightful blend of creamy chickpeas, rich tahini, and the flavorful addition of roasted red pepper. The touch of dill and vegetable and onion spice elevate the taste, creating a harmonious balance of flavors. Enjoy this dip as a wholesome appetizer, snack, or addition to any gathering. Its velvety texture and vibrant taste are sure to be a hit among your family and friends.

**FOR DIABETICS:** enjoy!

# Layered Taco Dip

## Ingredients:

- 1 can of refried beans
- 2 medium avocados, mashed
- Chopped/diced tomatoes and olives
- Small container of sour cream
- Taco seasoning (powdered spices), to taste
- Grated cheese (cheddar or Mexican blend)

## Instructions:

1. Begin by creating the bottom layer of the dip using the can of refried beans. Carefully spread the refried beans evenly at the bottom of your serving dish or in a suitable container.
2. For the next layer, take the 2 medium avocados and mash them until they are smooth and creamy. Spread the mashed avocados over the layer of refried beans, creating a flavorful and vibrant avocado base.
3. Proceed to add the chopped or diced tomatoes and olives as the next layer. Distribute them evenly over the avocado layer, creating a colorful and refreshing addition to the dip.
4. In a small bowl, mix the sour cream with taco seasoning to taste. Adjust the amount of seasoning based on your preference for spiciness. The seasoned sour cream layer will bring a creamy and zesty element to the dip.
5. Carefully spread the seasoned sour cream mixture over the tomato and olive layer, ensuring even coverage.
6. Finish off your layered taco dip by generously sprinkling grated cheese over the top. You can use cheddar cheese, Mexican blend, or any cheese that complements the flavors of a classic taco.
7. Your Layered Taco Dip is now complete and ready to be enjoyed. It showcases a medley of flavors and textures that capture the essence of a taco feast.
8. Serve your dip with an array of dippable options such as tortilla chips, vegetable sticks, or even toasted pita triangles.

Note: This Layered Taco Dip is a festive and crowd-pleasing appetizer that brings the flavors of tacos to a convenient and shareable format. Each layer contributes its unique taste and texture, resulting in a delicious and satisfying treat. Whether served at parties, gatherings, or casual get-togethers, this dip is sure to be a hit among guests who relish the flavors of a taco in every scoop.

**FOR DIABETICS:** enjoy with nut/seed crackers or Fresh Is Best taco chips!

# Cauliflower Cheese Breadsticks

## Ingredients:

- 1 cauliflower, ground in a food processor
- ½ cup mozzarella cheese, shredded
- ½ cup Parmesan cheese
- 1 large egg
- ½ tablespoon minced garlic
- ½ tablespoon fresh basil, finely chopped
- ½ tablespoon fresh parsley, finely chopped
- 1 teaspoon salt
- ½ teaspoon black pepper
- ¾ cup mozzarella cheese, shredded (for topping)

## Instructions:

1. Preheat your oven to 425°F (220°C). Line a baking sheet with parchment paper and set it aside.
2. Begin by preparing the cauliflower. Cut the cauliflower into florets and place them in a food processor. Pulse until the cauliflower is finely ground and resembles the texture of rice.
3. Transfer the ground cauliflower to a clean kitchen towel or cheesecloth. Squeeze out as much excess moisture as possible. This step is essential to ensure your breadsticks have the right consistency.
4. In a mixing bowl, combine the squeezed cauliflower with ½ cup of shredded mozzarella cheese, Parmesan cheese, a large egg, minced garlic, finely chopped fresh basil, finely chopped fresh parsley, salt, and black pepper. Mix well until all the ingredients are thoroughly combined.
5. Spread the cauliflower mixture evenly onto the parchment paper-lined baking sheet. Press it down to create a rectangle that's about ¼-inch thick. You can use a spatula to help shape it.
6. Bake the cauliflower mixture in the preheated oven for 10-12 minutes or until it starts to set and the edges become lightly golden.

7.  Remove the baking sheet from the oven and sprinkle the remaining ¾ cup of shredded mozzarella cheese evenly over the top.
8.  Return the baking sheet to the oven and bake for an additional 5-7 minutes, or until the cheese is melted and bubbly, and the edges are golden brown.
9.  Remove the cauliflower cheese bread from the oven and let it cool for a few minutes to set.
10. Using a sharp knife, cut the baked cauliflower mixture into breadstick-sized strips.
11. Serve your Cauliflower Cheese Breadsticks warm as a tasty and low-carb alternative to traditional breadsticks. They are delicious on their own or served with your favorite dipping sauces.
12. Enjoy your homemade Cauliflower Cheese Breadsticks that are not only flavorful but also a healthier choice for a satisfying snack or appetizer.

**FOR DIABETICS:** enjoy!

# Cauliflower English Muffins

## Ingredients:

- 2 cups cauliflower florets (about half a head of cauliflower)
- 1 egg
- 1 cup shredded mozzarella cheese (or any preferred cheese)
- 1/2 teaspoon dried oregano (or your favorite herb/spice)
- Salt and pepper to taste

## Instructions:

1. Preheat your oven to 375°F (190°C). Grease a muffin tin with cooking spray or line it with parchment paper to prevent sticking.
2. Start by making cauliflower rice. You can do this by grating the cauliflower florets on a box grater or using a food processor until it resembles rice-like grains.
3. Place the cauliflower rice in a microwave-safe bowl and microwave it for about 5-6 minutes or until it's cooked and softened. Alternatively, you can steam the cauliflower rice.
4. Allow the cooked cauliflower rice to cool for a few minutes. Then, place it in a clean kitchen towel or cheesecloth and squeeze out as much moisture as possible. Removing excess moisture is crucial to achieving a muffin-like texture.
5. Transfer the squeezed cauliflower rice to a mixing bowl. Add one egg, shredded mozzarella cheese, dried oregano (or preferred herb/spice), salt, and pepper. Mix everything together until well combined.
6. Divide the cauliflower mixture evenly among the muffin cups in the greased muffin tin. Press the mixture down with a spoon to compact it into each cup.
7. Bake the cauliflower "English muffins" in the preheated oven for approximately 20-25 minutes or until they become golden brown and set. They should have a muffin-like texture.
8. Remove the muffin tin from the oven and let the cauliflower "muffins" cool for a few minutes. Using a knife, gently loosen the edges to help remove them from the muffin tin.

9. Once they have cooled slightly, you can toast the cauliflower "muffins" in a toaster or under the broiler to achieve a more English muffin-like texture. Keep a close eye on them to prevent burning.
10. Serve your cauliflower "English muffins" as the base for your Eggs Benedict. Add a poached egg, ham or Canadian bacon, hollandaise sauce, and garnish with fresh parsley.

These cauliflower-based "English muffins" are a low-carb and gluten-free alternative that provides a tasty and nutritious base for your Eggs Benedict. Enjoy!

**FOR DIABETICS:** enjoy!

# Breakfast Egg Muffins

## Ingredients:

- 6 eggs
- ¼ cup cream
- ½ teaspoon salt
- ½ teaspoon pepper
- ½ teaspoon baking powder
- 1 cup chopped ham, bacon, or sausage (your choice)
- 1 cup shredded cheese (your choice, such as cheddar or mozzarella)
- Optional: diced zucchini, onion, asparagus, or any other veggies of your choice

## Instructions:

1. Preheat your oven to 350°F (175°C). Grease a muffin tin generously with butter or cooking spray to prevent sticking.
2. In a mixing bowl, crack the eggs and add the cream. Whisk them together until well combined.
3. Season the egg mixture with salt, pepper, and baking powder. Mix well to distribute the seasoning evenly.
4. Add your choice of chopped ham, bacon, or sausage to the egg mixture. If you want to include vegetables, add them now as well. Mix everything together to ensure even distribution.
5. Stir in the shredded cheese of your choice. The cheese will add flavor and create a delicious, cheesy texture.
6. Carefully pour or spoon the egg mixture into the buttered muffin tins. Fill each muffin cup about 2/3 full, allowing room for the muffins to rise as they bake.
7. Place the muffin tin in the preheated oven and bake for 25-30 minutes, or until the breakfast egg muffins are set and slightly golden on top. They should puff up and have a firm texture.
8. Remove the muffin tin from the oven and let the muffins cool for a few minutes.
9. Carefully use a butter knife or spoon to loosen the egg muffins from the muffin tin. They should come out easily due to the greased pan.

10. Serve your breakfast egg muffins warm as a delicious and convenient breakfast or snack option. They are perfect for on-the-go mornings or as a satisfying bite-sized treat.

Enjoy these Breakfast Egg Muffins with your favorite fillings and flavors. They are customizable and can be prepared ahead of time for a quick and easy meal or snack solution.

**FOR DIABETICS:** enjoy!

# Almond Flour Pancakes

## Ingredients:

- 2 eggs
- 1/3 cup almond milk
- 1/4 cup avocado oil
- 1 teaspoon vanilla extract
- 1 1/4 cups almond flour (or coconut flour)
- 1 teaspoon sweetener alternative (e.g., erythritol, stevia)
- Optional: 1/2 teaspoon vanilla extract
- 1/2 teaspoon baking powder
- Pinch of salt
- Cooking oil for the pan (about 4-inch rounds for easy flipping)
- Optional toppings: berries, sliced almonds, carob chips, dark chocolate chips

## Instructions:

1. In a blender, combine the eggs, almond milk, avocado oil, and 1 teaspoon of vanilla extract. Blend for about 5 seconds until well-mixed.
2. To the blender, add the almond flour (or coconut flour), sweetener alternative, and optional 1/2 teaspoon of vanilla extract.
3. If desired, add the baking powder and a pinch of salt to the blender. These ingredients will help your pancakes rise and provide a fluffy texture.
4. Blend all the ingredients together until you have a smooth pancake batter. The batter should be thick but pourable. If it's too thick, you can add a little more almond milk to reach your desired consistency.
5. Heat a non-stick skillet or frying pan over medium heat and add a small amount of cooking oil to coat the surface.
6. Using a ladle or measuring cup, pour about 1/4 cup of the pancake batter onto the hot skillet to form each pancake. You can adjust the size based on your preference, but keep them around 4 inches in diameter for easy flipping.

7. Cook the pancakes until you start to see bubbles forming on the surface and the edges become slightly browned, usually after about 2-3 minutes.
8. Carefully flip the pancakes using a spatula and cook for an additional 1-2 minutes on the other side until they are golden brown and cooked through.
9. If you'd like to add toppings like berries, sliced almonds, carob chips, or dark chocolate chips, you can sprinkle them onto the pancakes while they cook on the second side.
10. Once the pancakes are fully cooked and have a nice golden color, transfer them to a plate.
11. Serve your almond flour pancakes warm with your favorite toppings, such as fresh berries, a drizzle of sugar-free syrup, or a dollop of whipped cream if desired.

Enjoy these delicious, low-carb almond flour pancakes as a satisfying breakfast or brunch option that's both gluten-free and keto-friendly. They're a wholesome way to start your day with a touch of sweetness and flavor.

**FOR DIABETICS:** enjoy!

# Ritzza Pizza

## Ingredients:

- 1 cup rice (white, wild, brown, or a mix), cooked
- 2 cups water for white rice (or follow the package instructions)
- 2 ½ to 3 cups water for brown rice (or follow the package instructions)
- Cooking oil (for greasing the cookie sheet)
- Spaghetti sauce, pizza sauce, or alfredo sauce (your choice)
- Italian spice or pizza spice (to taste)
- Your favorite pizza toppings (e.g., meat, vegetables, pineapple)
- Your favorite cheese (grated or shredded)

## Instructions:

1. Cook the rice according to the package instructions, whether you're using white, wild, or brown rice. Make sure to rinse and drain the rice before adding the final water to cook.
2. Preheat your oven to 450°F (230°C).
3. Grease a large cookie sheet with cooking oil.
4. Spread the cooked rice evenly across the greased cookie sheet, covering the entire surface.
5. Pour your choice of sauce (spaghetti, pizza, or alfredo) over the rice, spreading it evenly.
6. Sprinkle Italian spice or pizza spice over the sauce according to your taste preferences. This adds flavor to the dish.
7. Add your favorite pizza toppings on top of the sauce-covered rice. Be creative and add whatever you enjoy to your pizza, whether it's meat, vegetables, pineapple, or other toppings.
8. Finally, generously sprinkle your favorite grated or shredded cheese over the top. You can use mozzarella, cheddar, parmesan, or any cheese you prefer.
9. Place the cookie sheet in the preheated oven and bake at 450°F (230°C) for about 15 minutes or until the cheese is bubbly and slightly browned.

10. Once the Ritzza Pizza is done, remove it from the oven and let it cool for a few minutes before serving.

Enjoy your homemade Ritzza Pizza, a creative and convenient way to enjoy pizza with a rice crust and your favorite toppings!

**FOR DIABETICS:** brown rice is better for your blood sugar levels, or use cauliflower rice.

# Zucchini Lasagna

## Ingredients:

- 1 pound ground beef, pork, or turkey
- 1 medium onion, chopped
- Mushrooms (optional), sliced
- 2-3 medium zucchinis, thinly sliced lengthwise (about 1/4-inch thick)
- 1 1/2 cups cottage cheese
- 2 cups shredded mozzarella cheese (or cheese of your choice)
- 1 can (24 ounces) of your favorite marinara or pasta sauce
- Salt and pepper to taste
- Italian seasoning or dried basil (optional for flavor)

## Instructions:

1. Preheat your oven to 450°F (230°C).
2. In a large skillet, brown the ground meat over medium heat. If using mushrooms and chopped onions, add them to the skillet and sauté until they're softened and the meat is fully cooked. Drain any excess fat.
3. Season the meat mixture with salt, pepper, and Italian seasoning or dried basil, if desired. Stir well to combine.
4. In a greased 9x13-inch baking dish, start layering the lasagna as follows:
5. Place a layer of thinly sliced zucchini on the bottom.
6. Spread half of the meat mixture evenly over the zucchini.
7. Spoon half of the cottage cheese over the meat.
8. Sprinkle half of the shredded mozzarella cheese on top.
9. Repeat the layers one more time, starting with another layer of zucchini slices.
10. Pour the marinara or pasta sauce evenly over the top layer of cheese.
11. Cover the baking dish with aluminum foil.
12. Bake in the preheated oven at 450°F (230°C) for about 35 minutes, or until the zucchini is tender and the lasagna is hot and bubbling.
13. Remove the foil and continue to bake for an additional 10 minutes or until the cheese on top is golden and bubbly.

14. Once done, remove the Zucchini Lasagna from the oven and let it cool for a few minutes before slicing and serving.

Enjoy your Zucchini Lasagna, a low-carb twist on the classic lasagna recipe that's loaded with flavor and veggies!

**FOR DIABETICS:** enjoy!

# Salsa

## Ingredients:

- 4 ripe tomatoes, chopped
- 4 cloves garlic, minced
- 3/4 white onion, finely chopped
- 1/4 green, yellow, or red bell pepper, finely chopped
- 2 tablespoons ground cumin (adjust to taste)
- 2 1/2 teaspoons lemon juice
- 2 teaspoons sea salt (adjust to taste)
- 2 tablespoons finely chopped fresh cilantro
- 1 teaspoon ground black pepper (adjust to taste)
- Optional: For hot salsa, add 1 serrano pepper (seeded and chopped); add 2 for fiery salsa.

## Instructions:

1. Prepare the Ingredients:
   - Start by washing and chopping the ripe tomatoes into small pieces.
   - Mince the garlic cloves finely.

- Finely chop the white onion and bell pepper.
- If you want your salsa to be spicy, you can add serrano peppers. Remember to seed them for milder heat or leave the seeds in for more spiciness.

2. Combine the Ingredients:
   - In a large mixing bowl, combine the chopped tomatoes, minced garlic, finely chopped onion, and bell pepper.
   - If you want to make your salsa spicy, add the chopped serrano peppers at this stage.

3. Season the Salsa:
   - Add the ground cumin, lemon juice, sea salt, chopped fresh cilantro, and ground black pepper to the bowl.
   - Adjust the seasoning to your taste preferences. You can add more cumin, salt, or pepper as needed.

4. Mix Well:
   - Gently toss all the ingredients together until well combined. Be careful not to crush the tomatoes; you want to maintain some texture.

5. Let It Rest:
   - Allow the salsa to sit for at least 30 minutes before serving. This time allows the flavors to meld and develop.

6. Serve or Store:
   - Divide the salsa into four portions or more, depending on your needs.
   - Serve immediately as a dip with tortilla chips, as a topping for tacos, grilled meats, or other dishes, or as an ingredient in your favorite recipes.
   - If you have leftovers, store them in an airtight container in the refrigerator. Homemade salsa is best consumed within a few days.

Enjoy your homemade salsa's vibrant flavors and adjust the heat level to your liking by adding more or fewer serrano peppers. It's a versatile and delicious addition to many dishes.

**FOR DIABETICS:** enjoy!

# Creamy Caesar Dressing

## Ingredients:

- 16 cloves garlic (optional, roasted with the skin on)
- 2 lemons
- 2 teaspoons Dijon mustard
- 2 teaspoons salt
- 1 teaspoon black pepper
- 1 cup olive oil
- 2-4 tablespoons whipped cream

## Instructions:

1. Roast the Garlic (Optional): Preheat your oven to 375°F (190°C). Place the unpeeled garlic cloves on a baking sheet and roast them for about 15-20 minutes or until they become soft and lightly browned. Remove from the oven and let them cool slightly. Once they're cool enough to handle, squeeze the roasted garlic cloves out of their skins.
2. Prepare the Lemons: Zest both lemons and then juice them.
3. Mix Ingredients: In a mixing bowl, combine the roasted garlic (if using), lemon zest, lemon juice, Dijon mustard, salt, and black pepper. Mix them together.
4. Add Olive Oil: Slowly drizzle in the olive oil while continuously whisking the mixture. This will help emulsify the dressing and make it creamy.
5. Adjust Consistency: Depending on how thick you want the dressing to be, add 2-4 tablespoons of whipped cream. Adjust the amount according to your preference for creaminess.
6. Taste and Adjust: Taste the dressing and adjust the seasoning, adding more salt, pepper, or lemon juice if needed.
7. Chill and Serve: Transfer the creamy Caesar dressing to an airtight container and refrigerate it for at least 30 minutes before using. Chilling allows the flavors to meld together.

Serve: Use your homemade creamy Caesar dressing to dress your favorite salads, especially Caesar salads. Drizzle it over crisp romaine lettuce, croutons, and grated Parmesan cheese for a classic Caesar salad experience.


## ROASTED GARLIC RECIPE:

### Ingredients:

- Whole garlic bulbs
- Olive oil
- Salt and pepper (optional)

### Instructions:

1. Prepare the Garlic Bulbs: Preheat your oven to 400°F (200°C). Take one or more whole garlic bulbs as needed. Ensure they are firm and not sprouting.
2. Trim the Tops: Use a sharp knife to trim about 1/4 to 1/2 inch off the top of each garlic bulb. This exposes the tops of the individual cloves.
3. Drizzle with Olive Oil: Place the trimmed garlic bulbs on a sheet of aluminum foil. Drizzle a small amount of olive oil over each bulb. You want enough oil to coat the cloves but not soak them.
4. Season (Optional): If desired, sprinkle a pinch of salt and pepper over the garlic bulbs for added flavor.
5. Wrap in Foil: Wrap each garlic bulb individually in the aluminum foil, ensuring they are tightly sealed.
6. Bake: Place the foil-wrapped garlic bulbs in the preheated oven directly on the oven rack or on a baking sheet. Roast for about 30-40 minutes. The garlic cloves should become soft and caramelized. You'll know they're done when they can be easily pierced with a fork.
7. Cool: Carefully remove the roasted garlic from the oven and let it cool for a few minutes. Be cautious, as it will be hot.
8. Extract the Cloves: Once cooled, gently squeeze the roasted garlic bulbs from the bottom. The softened cloves should pop out easily.

**FOR DIABETICS:** enjoy!

# Rosemary Garlic Potatoes

## Ingredients:

- 3 tablespoons olive oil
- 10 small red potatoes, quartered
- 1 tablespoon chopped fresh rosemary (or 1 teaspoon dried rosemary)
- ½ teaspoon salt (adjust to taste)
- ½ teaspoon black pepper (adjust to taste)
- ½ teaspoon finely chopped garlic (adjust to taste)

## Instructions:

1. Preheat Oven: Preheat your oven to 400°F (200°C).
2. Prepare Potatoes: Wash the small red potatoes thoroughly and cut them into quarters. Leave the skin on for added texture and flavor.
3. Toss with Seasonings: In a large mixing bowl, combine the quartered potatoes, olive oil, chopped rosemary, salt, black pepper, and finely chopped garlic. Toss everything together until the potatoes are evenly coated with the seasonings.
4. Arrange on Baking Sheet: Spread the seasoned potatoes out in a single layer on a baking sheet. Make sure they are evenly distributed to allow for even cooking.
5. Roast in the Oven: Place the baking sheet in the preheated oven and roast the potatoes for about 30-35 minutes, or until they are golden brown and crispy on the outside and tender on the inside. You can check for doneness by inserting a fork or knife into a potato piece; it should go in easily.
6. Serve: Remove the roasted rosemary garlic potatoes from the oven and transfer them to a serving dish. Serve hot as a delicious side dish to complement your main course.

**FOR DIABETICS:** enjoy!

# Red Lobster Biscuits

## Ingredients:

For the Biscuits:

- 2 cups all-purpose flour
- 1 tablespoon granulated sugar
- 1 tablespoon baking powder
- 2 teaspoons garlic powder
- 1/2 teaspoon salt
- 1/2 cup (1 stick) cold unsalted butter, grated
- 1 1/2 cups shredded sharp cheddar cheese
- 3/4 cup whole milk or buttermilk

For the Garlic Butter Topping:

- 3 tablespoons unsalted butter, melted
- 1/2 teaspoon dried parsley flakes
- 1/4 teaspoon garlic powder
- A pinch of salt

## Instructions:

1. Preheat the Oven: Preheat your oven to 450°F (230°C). Line a baking sheet with parchment paper or lightly grease it.
2. Mix Dry Ingredients: In a large mixing bowl, whisk together the all-purpose flour, granulated sugar, baking powder, garlic powder, and salt.
3. Add Cold Butter: Grate the cold unsalted butter using a box grater, and then add it to the dry ingredients. Mix the grated butter into the dry ingredients until the mixture resembles coarse crumbs.
4. Add Cheddar Cheese: Stir in the shredded sharp cheddar cheese until it's evenly distributed in the mixture.
5. Pour in Milk: Pour the whole milk into the bowl and stir until just combined. Be careful not to overmix; the dough should be slightly sticky.
6. Form Biscuits: Drop spoonfuls of biscuit dough onto the prepared baking sheet. You should get around 12 biscuits.

7. Bake: Place the baking sheet in the preheated oven and bake for about 10-12 minutes or until the biscuits are golden brown on top.

8. Prepare Garlic Butter Topping: While the biscuits are baking, prepare the garlic butter topping. In a small bowl, combine melted unsalted butter, dried parsley flakes, garlic powder, and a pinch of salt. Mix well.

9. Brush Biscuits: As soon as you remove the biscuits from the oven, brush the garlic butter mixture over the hot biscuits, ensuring they are well coated.

10. Serve Warm: Allow the biscuits to cool slightly before serving. Serve them warm and enjoy!

This is a homemade Red Lobster Cheddar Bay Biscuit copycat recipe. They are best served fresh out of the oven, and the cheesy, buttery, garlicky flavor is sure to satisfy your cravings.

**FOR DIABETICS:** not suggested.

# Cheddar Bacon Muffins

## Ingredients:

- 1 1/2 cups all-purpose flour
- 1 1/2 teaspoons baking powder
- 1/2 teaspoon baking soda
- 1/2 teaspoon salt and 1/4 teaspoon black pepper
- 1/4 teaspoon paprika
- 1/4 cup unsalted butter, melted
- 1 cup buttermilk
- 1 large egg
- 1 cup shredded sharp cheddar cheese
- 1/2 cup cooked and crumbled bacon (about 6 slices)
- 2 green onions, thinly sliced (optional flavor)

## Instructions:

1. Preheat your oven to 375°F (190°C). Line a muffin tin with paper liners or grease it well.
2. In a large mixing bowl, whisk together the flour, baking powder, baking soda, salt, black pepper, and paprika.
3. In a separate bowl, whisk together the melted butter, buttermilk, and egg until well combined.
4. Pour the wet ingredients into the dry ingredients and stir until just combined. Be careful not to overmix; a few lumps are okay.
5. Gently fold in the shredded cheddar cheese, crumbled bacon, and sliced green onions if using.
6. Spoon the muffin batter into the prepared muffin cups, filling each about two-thirds full.
7. Bake in the preheated oven for approximately 18-20 minutes or until the muffins are golden brown and a toothpick inserted into the center comes out clean.
8. Remove the muffins from the oven and let them cool in the muffin tin for a few minutes before transferring them to a wire rack to cool completely.

**FOR DIABETICS:** not suggested.

# Green Goddess Salad

## Ingredients:

For the Salad:

- 6 cups mixed salad greens (e.g., lettuce, spinach, arugula)
- 1 cup cherry tomatoes, halved
- 1/2 cucumber, sliced
- 1/4 cup red onion, thinly sliced
- 1/4 cup fresh herbs (e.g., basil, parsley, chives), chopped
- Optional: Avocado slices, croutons, or grilled chicken for added protein

For the Green Goddess Dressing:

- 1/2 cup mayonnaise
- 1/2 cup sour cream or Greek yogurt
- 1/4 cup fresh parsley, chopped
- 2 tablespoons fresh tarragon, chopped (or 2 teaspoons dried tarragon)
- 2 tablespoons fresh chives, chopped
- 1 green onion, chopped
- 2 cloves garlic, minced
- 1 tablespoon lemon juice
- 1 tablespoon white wine vinegar
- Salt and pepper to taste

## Instructions:

1. In a large salad bowl, combine the mixed greens, cherry tomatoes, cucumber, red onion, and fresh herbs.
2. In a blender or food processor, combine all the dressing ingredients: mayonnaise, sour cream or yogurt, fresh parsley, tarragon, chives, green onion, garlic, lemon juice, and white wine vinegar.

3. Blend the dressing until it's smooth and creamy. If the dressing is too thick, you can thin it out with a little water or additional lemon juice.
4. Season the dressing with salt and pepper to taste. Adjust the seasoning according to your preferences.
5. Pour the Green Goddess dressing over the salad ingredients. Start with a small amount and add more as needed. Toss the salad gently to coat it evenly with the dressing.
6. If desired, add avocado slices, croutons, or grilled chicken on top for extra flavor and protein.
7. Serve the Green Goddess salad immediately, garnished with extra fresh herbs if desired.

**FOR DIABETICS: enjoy!**

What did the grape say when
it got stepped on?

Nothing, it just let
out a little whine!

# Index

266

## BREAKFAST

## CASSEROLE

## COOKIES

## DESSERT

## DRINKS

## FISH

## POTATOES / PEROGIES

## SALAD

## SAUCES & DIPS

## SOUPS

# MESSAGE FROM THE AUTHOR

*I always enjoy my time over a meal! Conversing with my loved ones, friends, and associates. When your tummy is happy, your body, mind, and soul is happy!!!*

*Love To All who know me as*

*GiGi, Aunty Connie, or Dr. Constance Santego*

"What do you call a bear with no teeth?

A gummy bear!"

Shift happens...Create magic!
Dream BIGGER!

Dr. Constance Santego is a highly respected expert in the field of holistic health and spiritual healing. With over twenty-five years of experience teaching courses on these subjects, she has developed a deep understanding of the interconnectedness of the mind, body, and spirit in achieving overall well-being.

Dr. Santego holds a Ph.D. and Doctorate in Natural Medicine, which has provided her with a comprehensive understanding of alternative healing modalities and their application in promoting optimal health. Her educational background has equipped her with the knowledge to address health concerns from a holistic perspective, considering the physical, emotional, and spiritual aspects of an individual's well-being.

Throughout her career, Dr. Santego has been committed to sharing her knowledge and empowering others to take control of their health and healing. She has a unique ability to blend scientific research and traditional wisdom, creating a bridge between conventional and alternative medicine.

In her "Secrets of a Healer" educational series, Dr. Santego draws upon her vast experience and expertise to captivate readers with her insights and teachings. She takes readers on a transformative journey, delving into the realms of holistic health, spirituality, and self-discovery. Through her writing, she aims to inspire individuals to tap into their own innate healing abilities and embrace a balanced and harmonious approach to well-being.

Dr. Santego's work has touched the lives of many, guiding them toward a more profound understanding of themselves and their connection to the world around them. Her series serves as a beacon of wisdom, offering practical tools and techniques for personal growth and transformation.

Overall, Dr. Constance Santego's blend of knowledge, experience, and passion makes her a captivating figure in the field of holistic health and spiritual healing. Her contributions through teaching, writing, and her spellbinding series continue to inspire and empower individuals on their journeys toward well-being and self-discovery.

# ALSO AVAILABLE

Play the game *Ikona* – Discover Your Inner Genie

For additional information on

Dr. Constance Santego's

wide range of Motivational Products, Coaching Sessions,
Spiritual Retreats,
Live Events and Educational Programs

Go to

www.ConstanceSantego.ca

Follow on Instagram - Constance_Santego and
Facebook - constancesantego

Subscribe and receive Free Information and Meditations on my
YouTube Channel - Constance Santego

CONSTANCE SANTEGO

CONSTANCE SANTEGO

www.ingramcontent.com/pod-product-compliance
Lightning Source LLC
Chambersburg PA
CBHW061140120626
46546CB00005B/1861